Petals of Rain

A Mother's Memoir

Rica Keenum

To my boys,
who are the very substance of my heart.

My love for you is boundless.

Author's Note:

Memory, pain and healing move organically. Emotions come in waves. That's why *Petals of Rain* is not a conventional book. I chose to capture my story in a nonlinear fashion, weaving the past and present together. It started with a series of essays, none of which revealed my dysfunctional childhood. That was a heavy box I'd always preferred to keep stowed away. But as the story unfolded, it was clear that I had to unpack a few things. It was vital to the narrative.

I had to go back to move forward.

What I learned helped me understand who I was and the decisions that altered my path. Researchers say early trauma can shape a victim's brain, affect the formation of neural pathways and cause long-term guilt, shame, depression and low self-esteem. Like a venomous snake bite, the poison swims through our veins. It reshapes our hearts, our hopes, our needs, our beliefs about ourselves and the world. It can strangle our voices for a time, but it cannot silence us forever.

To those who ache today, I can only say this: You are not your trauma. You are not your wound. You are not your failures. You are not too small, too weak, too insignificant to count. You are everything you pray, wish, dare, choose to be. You are a petal of rain, a glorious, glistening drop. And together, we are a beautiful storm.

THE RAINY DAY

The day is cold, and dark, and dreary;
It rains, and the wind is never weary;
The vine still clings to the moldering wall,
But at every gust the dead leaves fall,
And the day is dark and dreary.

My life is cold, and dark, and dreary;
It rains, and the wind is never weary;
My thoughts still cling to the moldering past,
But the hopes of youth fall thick in the blast,
And the days are dark and dreary.

Be still, sad heart! and cease repining;
Behind the clouds is the sun still shining;
Thy fate is the common fate of all,
Into each life some rain must fall,
Some days must be dark and dreary.

~ Henry Wadsworth Longfellow

Chapter 1

Petals of Rain

Drip

I don't know how old I am, only that my feet don't touch the floor when we sit on the creaking porch swing. Grandma's warm body next to mine, I watch a sword of white lightning cut through the dark sheet of sky. The rain trickles down slowly at first, like a timid tap dancer on the massive stage of the earth. Mesmerized, we listen as the tapping gains momentum and then roars to a full-bodied downpour. Grandma puts her hand on my knee as if to signal her pleasure. The cool air tastes like a spring bouquet, sweet and dewy. I fall in love with the rain that night, the way you fall in love with anything ethereal — with a sunrise or the sound of your grandmother's voice.

Drop

When I am seven years old, we live in a small house in Wisconsin. My siblings and I shack up in a room with a bunk bed. We have no space to twirl or play tag, nowhere to spread out or dance. A library copy of *The Wind in The Willows* in my hands, I inhale the scent of ink on glossy pages and imagine I am the mole in the story, escaping my stifling hole in the ground and finding a rowboat at the edge of a river. My younger brother dangles from the top bunk; his wormy arms are wrapped around the cherry wood rail. The room is dense with adolescent sweat and the heat of too many bodies. My sister lies with her Walkman, the sounds of the 80s piping in her ears. Every so often, we part the curtains to look out at the gray sky. The rain is a relentless drummer, striking a beat on the window. We are the captains of exploration, longing to steer our bicycle-ships in the sunshine, to wield stick-swords in the yard and steal apples from the neighbor's tree. But the rain has screwed up the whole clan of kids who normally linger outdoors: Chris, R.J., Dee Dee and Danny. At some point as we sulk, My mom peeks her head in our tiny stale bedroom and holds out our swimming suits.

"Let's go," she commands.

We peel off our clothes and slide on our suits. Hopping over the rumpled heaps of our clothing, we trample out the door and into the rain. My feet slap like little oars in the warm puddles on the asphalt driveway. I throw back my head and open my mouth — wide like a hungry bird. I taste the iridescent jewels of rain on my tongue and note the rainbow, shimmering like a wish in the dark of our sky.

***

I am a scrawny young girl with hair half as big as my body. I sit on the cracked cement steps where the sun paints shapes through the trees. I lick the sticky remnants of a Popsicle off my fingers and forearm and watch the cars pass on the narrow street beyond the sidewalk. I refuse to leave the steps to wash because my dad is coming — any minute he'll be here.

He will.
He will.

Last time he showed up, I rode in the back of his car with my siblings. A man on the radio sang about an itsy bitsy, teenie weenie yellow polka dot bikini. My dad sang along, and we three kids giggled and howled at the word "weenie." We went to the toy store and I picked out a doll with yarn braids and round cheeks like plastic peaches. But now I squeeze my eyes shut and try to imagine my dad. I wish my vision to life again and again until I learn there is no magic in wishing. My mother said he's worthless anyway.

On another day, I watch my friend's father teach her to swim. He coaxes her into the water, his broad hand sweeps across the cool, shadowy lake. I watch the water ripple in the shine of his eyes. He reaches for my friend as she flails, and I want it to be me. I want to be the girl a father reaches for. It will never be me.

***

We're playing in our bedroom when my mom opens the door and leans against the frame. Her makeup is bright and shimmery; her hair is teased to perfection and frozen in place, an Aqua Net dream. I have a rainbow sticker in my fingers and I'm contemplating where to put it: on the dresser, on the bunk bed, on my pant leg or my shirt? My brother and sister are here too, doing equally important work with their toys as we wait for Mom's date to arrive.

"I want you to call him Dad from now on," she tells us, "so people don't look at us funny." She steps back into the hall and shuts the door.

Later she changes my name. And I'm not Mexican anymore. Instead I'm white like my new dad.

I am 12 years old when I see her from Grandma's window on the day when secrets hang in the air. I don't know if I'll ever need her more. *It's over now,* I think. *Her love is mine at last.*

She wears a blue fur coat that smells of perfume, cigarettes and chewing gum: the bouquet of her. The bouquet of my mother. Five years of his aftershave rubbed body at my bedside, hot whispers in my ear, serpent hands beneath my blankets. Some nights I hid in the bathtub, but when I tried to sleep, I found his naked silhouette stamped on my eyelids. And in the daylight, I carried the hard stone of that secret, and I practiced the way I would tell it. But when I opened my mouth, the words were too heavy for my tongue. Now she knows. Social workers in navy suits flit about as if there are pieces of glass on the floor. I'm certain I'll never see the man again. Is this not enough to break a marriage?

I hear Mom's high heels on the concrete. She steps inside and I wait for her eyes to find me, but I'm invisible. She's angry. I see anger all over her, like chafed skin. When she finally turns to me, I am desperate to prove my case.

"I swear on the Bible it's true," I sputter.

"Don't be stupid," she snaps.

Stupid, stupid me.

But she likes this option — ignorance. It is the answer she can live with while still living with the man. Two systems fail, first parental then legal. We attend court-ordered counseling and then I'm back home again, with her, with him. I am the girl who learns to un-tell her secrets. And this is what I know: If I want a perfect family, I'll have to make my own.

Chapter 2

Two Leaves

My teen years come like a cyclone. Taking a girl's voice is the same as taking her power. I do what I can to feel powerful. Some days I walk into high school and exit through the back, too sad to endure the day in classrooms swarming with kids. Kids who are smarter. Kids who play soccer. Kids who aren't cracked like me. I walk several miles, the wind clawing at my throat. When I get home, the house is empty and quiet. I curl into bed, into the blankets, into my own emptiness. Into the womb of dreams.

I don't have a single friend who is genuinely happy at home. Is this the disease of teenhood or the footprint of parental rejection? One girl's parents are in jail, so she's stuck with her grandma, a cranky woman with an ashtray of a voice. Another girl's mother lives across town with her no-good boyfriend. She rents my friend a separate apartment, which at the time seems very cool, but later I realize is not. When the woman appears at the apartment after fights with her boyfriend, my friend screams at her mother with an unbelievable hatred, the voice of the abandoned. I watch her snarl, a wounded cat hissing in a corner.

At 16, I love-hate my mother and find new ways to run away from home, to sneak into a friend's bedroom window and sleep in her moldy closet, next to empty bottles of peach schnapps. Endless bottles. I think my friend is an alcoholic. When my mother finds me, she drags me back home where dad-monster threatens to cut off my long hair. I'm in the kitchen, jammed between the fridge and the wall, his cigarette breath on my face, hot spittle on my cheek. My sister lunges at him from behind.

"Cut her hair and I'll cut your throat, you son of a bitch."

My sister: seventeen with a baby. Pills down her throat because she wants out of this too.

***

My friends and I listen to loud music in basements, go to parties, concerts, festivals. We dance like we're shaking off heartbreak and chug 40-ounce beers until our stomachs go sour and we find the courage to scream. I am working full time at a department store and searching for the next new thing. A plaid mini skirt with a sale tag, a fad diet, a song that resonates with my soul or someone to hold my hand. And then comes J. He is the worst kind of cliché — tall, dark and handsome, chivalrous, too. His hair is electric black. When he smiles at me from a gas station in Milwaukee, I fumble to let down the car window. The air is too thick to breathe.

"He's the hottest guy I have ever seen in real life," I will tell my sister the next day. I am 18 and being "hot" is a virtue. Inside my green Plymouth Duster, a few friends spur me on. From the counter where he stands eyeing me through the glass, he motions for me to come inside the store. He then tells me to call him "J" and slides his phone number across the counter. It's just an ordinary scrap of paper, but I tuck it down into my jeans pocket as far as I can shove it. I sense he is a part of my future, but for better or worse — I can't tell.

Within a few weeks, he is sending roses to my work and buying me silk pajamas — lavender shorts and a matching top, feminine enough to flatter me but not sexy enough to scare me off.

We walk together beneath the winking moon, inhaling the cool of the night and each other, our stories and scents. He says his mother dabbled in drugs and brought home some wicked boyfriends. When she cooked for them, he sat hungry, waiting for a taste. When he turned 16, he snagged a job at Burger King and served up fries and chicken nuggets. "One for them, two for me," he demonstrates, opening his beautiful mouth like a hungry bear. I throw my head back and laugh. Sometimes we laugh until my face hurts, or we sink into soft blankets and watch movies in the dark. Every so often, he leans in my direction and asks if I'm thirsty, hungry, comfortable. "Need another pillow?"

We talk until the sun nudges into the room. I tell him about my memories, the way they flicker like a half-screwed bulb, surprising me with scenes from the past. He likes this about us. "We're different," he says, and it seems like the best thing to be. To be like him, to be near him, the boy with the movie star face. He tells me they don't know rejection like we do, and I feel this statement, right down to my scars. My shame rises up to applaud. An internal standing ovation. How many times have I thought, *I'm the only one here who is damaged. Stupid, stupid me.*

To be loved is good, but to be understood is everything. J takes my hand and weaves his fingers around mine. We are two leaves clumped together after a storm.

***

7

J takes me to every restaurant in the city: sticky pancake houses, Italian eateries with oil-soaked bread and waterfront places where the view puts patrons in a trance. We celebrate every day with food. This is his currency of love. He brings me chocolate cupcakes with white frosted curls and loops. He learns how I take my coffee, then hands me a steaming paper cup, cream no sugar. He buys me T-shirts that fit me just right. He studies me as if for a test. I am his favorite subject. He knows my favorite songs, colors, flowers, books, movies, shoes, nail polish, everything, everything, everything. And in this way, he makes me feel like I am everything — until the day I am nothing.

***

After a string of good weeks together, we drive to Grant Park and I show J the walking paths, strewn with golden leaves. It's the most glorious place. "My aunt used to bring me here," I say, smiling at the memory of us skittering over rocks and up the hilly patches, hand in hand. In some places, the path was steep, and I could look down and see a glassy creek cutting through the green expanse like a silver snake wriggling in the grass.

We study the trees and their web of branches, the way they reach out like fingers yearning to touch. "You have to see the covered bridge," I urge, pulling J along. When we find the weathered structure, we marvel at its arch and the message etched overhead: *Enter these woods and view the haunts of nature.*

We find a picnic area and sit, listening to the sounds of families in the distance, kids playing tag and parents cracking open coolers packed with soda cans and sandwiches. We laugh when we see a single guy hovering over a pizza, the greasy box on a blanket in the shade.

"He's gonna eat the *whole* pizza," I say. "How romantic."

"I ate a large pizza once — right on the sidewalk," J says. "I bought it with my own money and I didn't want to take it home and share it." We laugh until he stands up, smoothes out his jeans and announces, "We're going for pizza."

***

J has something to say. "It would be an honor if you moved in with me." He's extra chivalrous today —Rhett Butler straight from the pages of my paperback. He shares a house with his older sister and her children. I am living here and there, and I like his offer.

I move into the upstairs bedroom that is cozy and bright, but I am still too shy to undress in front of him, so I yank off my work clothes in our closet as I peek through the slats in the painted louver doors. The sun shimmers in through the half-opened window and J sits entranced by the television. He's watching a basketball game and I hear the cheering crowds as athletes stampede toward the ball. I emerge from the closet wearing a baggy T-shirt that hovers just above my knees— his shirt, which I have adopted for leisurely after-noons. I sit down beside him and pretend to care about the men and the plays and the points. But all that really matters is the weight of his hand on my thigh.

When his niece and nephew appear in the hall and start to make noise, I watch J get up swiftly and toss the television remote on my lap. Through the open bedroom door, I see him hovering over the two big-eyed kids in their cotton pajamas. They pause, toys dangling at their sides, and J's arms go out like a pair of wings. He scoops them up and piles them on the carpet. His hands go wild, tickling and poking their little bod-ies as they whoop and squirm. This, I decide, is the quality I like best in a man.

The next day plays out differently. I come home to find my clothes flung all over the lawn — my dresses draped over shrubs and my jeans in rumpled mounds on the sidewalk. My books, dog-eared volumes of poetry and musty, thrift-store classics, are stacked in a box near the stoop. It is like I am stepping into a haphazard yard sale. I make my way toward the bedroom as if I'm entering the house for the first time. I see J on the bed. His eyes are mud puddles, dark and shadowy. I have a sense that I don't know him, as if we are meeting all over again. I search for the light on his face, but I am staring at a blackout.

"What is this about?" I ask feebly. But J is far away, unable to be reached by my voice.

I stay with a friend for the night and when I return the following day, all of my clothes are in the closet again. My books are in our bedroom where they belong. J's fit has come and gone so quickly, I barely have time to process it. And when he smiles, it is hard to believe it happened at all.

Later, J's sister lets me in on a secret: he was angry because he saw me talking to the men next door, a simple greeting as I headed to my car. I thought it was nothing at all, but when she tells me this, I instinctively question myself, wondering how the scene might have appeared to J from the window. Did I get too close, laugh too hard at something one of the men said? There's a red flag here, flapping fierce and bright. But I'm too young, too naive and too in love to see it.

***

At the library, I find the book *Men Are from Mars, Women Are from Venus: The Classic Guide to Understanding the Opposite Sex*. I can be understanding. I need to be more understanding.

J and I have become inseparable. We do everything and nothing at all. Some nights we just drive with the windows down and the tingle of night on our skin. I watch his face light up behind the beams of oncoming cars as we streak by at high speeds. Our laughter spills into the dark. If it were just the two of us in the world, that would be enough.

"I can see us married," he says. And when I close my eyes, I see it too.

I am 18, he's 19 and we don't know much but we think we know love, so we make it official at Chapel of the Bells just three months later. It's a charming little sanctuary in the heart of the south side, reminiscent of a Wordsworth poem: a violet by a mossy stone, half-hidden from the eye. I wear a simple white dress I found on sale for $40. J wears a rented suit, black with a pair of Nikes. I laugh when I see the shoes. He is sleek, sophisticated, hands crossed in front of his buttoned-up tux. And then the shoes — are they an expression of style or a symbolic statement: I won't grow up. Not now, not ever.

Chapter 3

A Son

At 20, I should have been procrastinating college homework, sipping something cheap and fizzy or trying on jeans at the mall. Instead, I am at home coiled on the bed and bulging at my middle, stroking the globe of my belly, the new world beneath my fingers. There isn't anywhere else I want to be. I hadn't tried for a baby, but when I realize why I've been so exhausted, why my body suddenly feels like a balloon filled with sand, why I can't stop peeing — I am intrigued. When I share my news with J, we are standing outside watching the road in front of the house. Without warning, the words fly out of my mouth and into the cool autumn air.

"I'm pregnant."

I'm not so much telling him as I am telling myself, tasting the phrase on my tongue — hearing my prelude to motherhood, which in turn will mean midnight feedings, emotional chaos, sleep deprivation, temporary insanity and throwing small parties for first-time toilet poopers. Before the ease of Google, I arm myself with a library card. My penchant to understand all the specifics in detail leaves me bug-eyed and hunched over textbooks, absorbed in the anatomy and physiology of childbirth. I examine the glossy photos of somersaulting fetuses swimming like shrimp in murky seas of amniotic fluid. I learn about burping, bathing, weaning, training and when the first teeth should cut through the gums. I join a Dr. Seuss book club, quit caffeine and sip herbal tea while quietly contemplating our future. At night I dream of my child, of the silk of his skin and the tiny pearls of his fingers and toes. When I can only lie comfortably on my side, his spastic kicks and jabs jolt me into groggy fits of sleep. One night he kicks so ferociously, I imagine his gangly, brown foot burrowing through my lower belly. Before I even know he is a he, and that his skin will be a chestnut shade of brown like his dad's, I envision the foot, bearing a fuzzy, blue bootie.

In my third trimester, a nurse hands me a black-and-white photo of his ghostly form. It is not like looking at a perfect stranger, a distant cousin or someone I will meet soon enough. It is like seeing the one I already know, if only in flutters and thumps — the spirited little man who marches inside my abdomen, and who will march into my life with the same vigor. Throughout my pregnancy, I keep a journal of poetry and musings, mostly crappy poems that seem eloquent at the time. They've long since been lost in various moves to apartments, duplexes and houses. And while I don't recall the lines, I do remember the title of the very first poem I wrote for my son, "I Don't Know You, But I Love You."

***

The pain is dull, a low kick at the base of my spine that started in the early morning while I was still in bed watching daylight creep in. It's Sunday, so we lounge around a while in our pajamas and I wait for the cramping to either lessen or worsen.

I'm okay with either because at this point I am tired of lumbering around like a beanbag chair with limbs. After some hours of assessing the pain, I realize these are more than Braxton Hicks contractions, the sporadic "false" labor cramps all the books say are practice. We should probably head to the hospital.

"It's gonna be a while," a nurse tells us after we arrive. "First babies like to take their time." The hospital is packed because for some reason, every baby in the city has decided to make its entrance today. "There won't be a room ready for hours and you'll be more comfortable at home," the nurse explains. I waddle back to the car with my stupefied husband, meticulously packed bag and swollen everything.

I spend the next few hours in the bathtub. My belly is a tugboat in a bath of warm bubbles. Then pink-cheeked and shriveled, I walk around the nursery, picking up all the baby items in the whimsical, wallpapered room: a plush Winnie the Pooh bear, sealed bottles of lotion and oil, diapers as small as a deck of playing cards stacked in the animal-faced diaper rack. I sit in the thrift-store chair I'd scrubbed with upholstery cleaner, run my fingers on its gray, velvet fabric and let my hand wander to the wicker side table where a radio sits with a tape locked and loaded: Baby's First Bible Songs. Motherhood is making me oddly religious, more so than I ever imagined. I'm desperate to give this child everything good in the world and terrified to know that I can't. I've begun, in the smallest ways, to reach out for help. I crank up *"Jesus Loves Me"* and hope that he does. Love me, but more importantly, my baby.

When we finally return to the hospital, it's a few hours later and the pain has reached epic proportions. As we hurry inside, I decide that if they don't have a room, I'll take a goddamn desk, table or mattress on the floor in the hallway. But they have a room. I fling myself on the bed, dizzy and in a state of quiet shock. I try to recall what I read during the months I crammed for this — the labor and delivery exam. The baby books said there'd be uterine muscle spasms. The cervix would dilate to ten centimeters. In the second stage of labor, kneeling on all fours might help to relieve the backaches. It sounded reasonable when I read it, but right now it seems utterly ridiculous. I am panting, sweating, clawing at the bedsheets. Everything I read over the past nine months is a fairytale now. The medical terms, the pregnancy guides, colorful charts and diagrams. And the anatomical images — those were other women's bodies. They belonged to science. But this was happening to me, and it was not colorful like the books.

Shortly after 4 a.m., baby KJ comes — 6 pounds, 10 ounces, 20 inches long. He feels shockingly small and I can't do the math. All that belly for this? It's like I've unwrapped a giant box to find a coin inside. But he is beautiful, and not just because mothers are supposed to say that. I marvel at his tiny bones, wrapped in the wrinkled satin of fresh skin, his hair is slick black and sprouting everywhere. When he opens his mouth to squeal, his lips quiver like guitar picks, strumming the chords of my heart.

***

I don't have friends anymore. My life is not mine alone, and it's both wonderful and wearisome. I have a baby and a husband and I watch *Mister Rogers' Neighborhood*. I take the stroller out for a spin on warm days. We walk eight blocks to my grandma's house, through the old neighborhood where two-bedroom ranches squat on tiny green lots. These are the streets I walked to school, with familiar trees and sidewalk cracks, windows I peered through in passing. I gawked at the occupants inside, attempting to assemble their families as if mentally playing house. It seemed I never stopped wondering about other families. Were they happy? Did they have secrets too? In school, I daydreamed about living in a sitcom family: The Seavers, The Cunninghams, The Bradys. I tried on other parents, imagining they were mine: fathers who scurried into the school office with bagged lunches for kids who forgot, mothers who helped chaperone field trips, enduring sweltering bus rides with riotous preteen mobs.

My aunt never had her own children, so on weekends I was hers, if only from Friday to Sunday. She'd hand me a plastic cup at Grant Park and I'd run free, on the hunt for chipmunks, baby bunnies or anything cute and cuddly. I never caught any critters, but the thrill of the chase was enough. On the damp banks of a pond, my aunt held my hand and we watched in wonder as an otter bobbed and splashed in the water.

"There he is again," she shouted as I cheered. We'd named the otter "Emmet," like the one in the story she read me, *Emmet Otter's Jug Band Christmas.*

Picnics in the park, puzzles in front of the fireplace — this was the stuff of families. With my aunt and my grandparents, I collected enough good memories to equalize the bad.

At the corner, I stop to adjust the stroller and a feeling overwhelms me. It is the excitement I always feel when nearing Grandma's house. I'm a mama with a baby, but my heart feels five years old. I want ice cream and cartoons, storybooks and songs, grandma petting my knee.

When I arrive at the yellow door, I maneuver the stroller inside. I make my way through the front room, past the end tables with marble tops and brassy handles. Past the porcelain baby lamb that bears her favorite Bible verse, "The Lord is my shepherd, I shall not want." I see her on the sofa, leaning forward, her face cocked toward the sound of us. When she sees me with my brand-new son, her eyes flutter with emotion. I know she's been waiting for us.

I collapse beside her. Motherhood is kicking my ass. She coos at my son then takes him onto her lap with the ease of a seven-time mother, which she is. Within moments, her fragrance has engulfed his blanket and his cheeks are scalloped with her lipstick. We glance at reruns of *Murder She Wrote*, and I tell her how hard it has been with the sleepless nights and projectile vomit. My husband doesn't seem to comprehend my stress. She reaches over and gently pinches a plump sweet infant leg. She is a woman at the market, marveling at the freshest batch of produce.

"A man can work from sun to sun, but a woman's work is never done," she says.

It's the loveliest phrase I've ever heard, simply because I am desperate for validation. I watch my grandma as she admires KJ. I see shelter in the familiar folds of her face and in her smile. I want to crawl inside those folds, where the weight of everything can't crush me. But I settle for this spot next to her, as close as I can get on the floral sofa where we used to watch *Scooby Doo*. She reaches out and squeezes KJ's leg again. Her spotty hand. His new skin. She can't get enough. I close my eyes and inhale deeply. It feels like my first breath since his birth.

***

A cartoon theme song has been stuck in my head for a week, so I pop a Jewel CD in the stereo and serenade KJ. "You were meant for me, and I was meant for you…" I belt it out so hard his face goes flat, then I bounce him on my hip and swirl him around the room. These are my kind of dance parties. When I'm too dizzy to stand, we flop on the bed in front of the open window. I watch the cars go by and wait for J to pull up in our

Plymouth — the next big event in my lonely life. Only, it's not. I hear his feet on the stairs and then he appears in his grimy work clothes. He sits in front of the television, sweat beads glistening at his temples. When I ask if he's hungry, he mumbles not now and turns up the volume on Sports Center.

When the weekend comes, I pack sandwiches in a cooler. A bag of chips and bottles of juice and water. We have a blanket and a diaper bag. We're headed for the lake. I sit in the backseat where I can be close to KJ, who is strapped in his car seat, sandaled feet thrashing in the breeze. I still haven't learned how to step away from my child. I spend my days observing him like a scientist and making lists of everything: hours slept, ounces eaten, diapers dirtied in a day. I read up on developmental milestones, collect endless parenting books. It's a good thing the internet is not yet mainstream.

J turns down the radio and finds me in his rearview. "Everything okay back there?" he asks. His face is serene and bright, his smile an upturned rainbow. We are happy today, ready for an adventure. I give him a thumbs up and we drive east until the blue sky meets the ripple of the lake. We turn onto the main drag where the whole city spins and throbs. Cyclists cruise by in neon shorts and rollerbladers glide through the crowds. Dogs pull their leashes taut and drag their wet tongues in the heat. Kids climb the jagged rocks along the shore. It takes a while to find a spot to park, but we have a while. We have all day and we plan to use it — I hope.

Today is a rare day in which J is neither at work nor dormant in front of the television, hypnotized by a speeding ball. He wriggles KJ from his seat and we take to the sidewalk, blanket and cooler in hand. With each step, we get further from our routines and I feel myself lifting, no longer weighted by the lists and books, the pursuit of parental perfection. With the incandescent sun on our skin, everything sparkles.

J bounces KJ as we walk, then stops, slides him up his torso and nibbles his belly. I watch KJ's little arms windmilling with excitement in the sky that's blue as a dream. When we find the perfect spot, a grassy plot beneath an outstretched tree, we fling our blanket open and smooth the corners down.

We lie on our backs and watch the clouds puff past like the seedy heads of dandelions. KJ's foot pokes up and J grabs it in his fist, rolls onto his side and examines it then holds it against his lips for a long, slow kiss.

Chapter 4

Round Two

When KJ is a toddler, I discover I'm pregnant again. My first inkling comes not with a test strip but with an insatiable craving. We are grocery shopping on a Sunday when I place a plastic bowl of chopped fruit in the shopping cart. I am eyeing it as we maneuver through the store and J takes his sweet time choosing cereal, cuts of beef, cartons of juice. My hands nearly shake as I fight the urge, aisle after aisle, to rip off the lid and drill into the bowl. I lick my lips, fix my gaze on my little package of fresh fruit: plump red watermelon, jewels of grapes, golden cuts of cantaloupe. As we check out, the cashier is slow and chatty. She engages KJ and this is the one time in which I don't care to hear how handsome my son is. How stunning his curls are. Let's get this show on the road.

In the parking lot, it's all too much to bear. The sun melts onto my shoulders and I am parched. I hunch over the shopping cart as J loads bags into the trunk. When he turns to grab the last of them, his face registers shock at the sight of me, cheeks fat with cold fruit, forearms dripping with watermelon juice. Nothing has ever tasted so good. I chew, chew, chew, then swallow. Breathe hard then say, "I think I might be pregnant."

***

The ultrasound said it's a boy and we're glad KJ will have a brother. I take a job at a Super America gas station across the street from our apartment, which is a nice enough place in a good neighborhood. We need the extra cash and I like getting out of the house. I work evenings after J comes home from his day shift, which means we spend only minutes together most days. Some nights I look up from the lottery machine and see J under the shine of streetlights with KJ on his hip and a foil-wrapped plate in his hand. He stands in line while I slide cartons of cigarettes and Quick Picks across the counter and joke with the neighborhood customers.

"If you hit it big with these numbers, remember the nice girl who sold you the ticket."

"Scouts honor," the man replies, straightening his stance for a three-finger salute.

When J approaches, he plunks down a plate of hot buttered noodles and green beans or Tuna Helper he whipped up from the box. Later, I scarf it down in the back room while watching the cameras for customers. Then I head outside to empty the trash bins. By 9 p.m., each of the six garbage cans will be an Eiffel Tower of Styrofoam cups, candy wrappers and greasy fast food bags. Chasing trash across the lot is especially fun on windy nights or when ice spreads out like tentacles. On the night before I give birth again, I make my rounds with aching feet and heave the bulging bags onto my belly before taking a deep breath and tossing them into the stinky dumpster behind the building. I go home and soak my swollen legs in a hot bath.

On Friday morning, I watch the snow outside my window and think about how long it will take J to leave work, slosh through this mess and get me to the hospital. I don't want to call him too early and get sent home like we did the first time. When another pain shoots through me, I know it's time to act.

I pick up the phone and dial J's work number, fingers mashing with a force that surprises me. My body has become irate. Before he picks up, there is a pause in which I sit with the phone cradled on my shoulder, waiting. My breath comes out hard, a husky fog in my ear. When J fumbles on the line, I tell him to get home now.

"Are you sure?" he asks.

"Yes," I say, holding the "S" on my tongue so that it slides out, sharp. A hiss.

I get to the hospital too late — no time for an epidural. The staff whisks me off in a wheelchair, tosses a cotton gown in my lap and draws the curtain. The pain is so great I want to stop, drop and roll out the fire that is blazing at the base of my spine. Have I entered a sci-fi movie? Is this an alien or a baby boy? I imagine a one-eyed bundle of teeth and talons slashing through my flesh.

"I *need* something for the pain," I tell the nurse, who is helping me into the adjustable bed. I squeeze her hand a bit too hard just to drive home the point. She nods, walks away and a few more hospital employees come in, bustle about, poke my arm and thread me with tubes and bags. The pain lingers but it's strangely diffused, a vapor in my belly. The nurse explains as she reaches for my arm, "I could only give you something mild. You're just so close."

This is a whole new experience. During KJ's marathon birth, an anesthesiologist came in and ushered me to the edge of the bed where I bent over and showed him my spine. He jabbed a needle in, and voila! My lower half went numb. A semi could have parked on my lap and I'd have smiled and said, "No problem." But now I have *something mild*, and mild it is.

I am squinting through the pain, scowling at the room. I count the stupid faces bobbing around my bed. Stupid, stupid faces. My husband is in the lobby watching ESPN. He doesn't have the stomach for this, so I will give birth without him again. At least this time he's not going home to sleep.

The doctor shows his stupid face shortly before the baby comes. "Push" is all he can concoct, this medically trained robot who stands at the foot of my bed in a silk shirt and pressed pants, a stethoscope dangling from his neck like a noose just out of my reach. "One more push," he repeats monotonously until I finally call bullshit.

"LIAR!" I howl, arms banging on the mattress. But I continue to push on command and finally, after too many "one last pushes," a son oozes out. He is crimson faced with a roaring mouth and fists like sturdy knobs. His head is plump and swirled with hair and when I reach for him, he lands in my arms with a thunk.

Aside from J and KJ, my aunt is my only visitor. She brings warm chocolate chip cookies to the hospital, sits in the vinyl chair next to my bed and congratulates me. She smells like Jean Nate and I imagine the bottle with its shiny black bauble for a top. As a young girl, I spied her perfumes while she filled my bath with bubbles and toys: Red Door, Chloe and Liz Claiborne. They are ornaments in my memory now, glimmering on the knotty branches of the past. When she leans in for a kiss goodbye, I take a long whiff and savor her, then watch her go, resisting the urge to reach out.

***

At home, we admire the chubby new baby boy. He is an ocean of waves in his tight blue onesie. The sleeves are too short and his head pokes out of the neckline and bobs like a tethered balloon. KJ is a proud two-year-old brother. He drapes a big-boy arm around the baby. What a pair. When they lie on the bed together, their black hair tangles like licorice twists. J is back at work and I have a few weeks to recover. Our apartment feels like a yawn, tedious and dry with a stifling heat that exhales through the vents. The baby swing clicks back and forth, and I watch my son swoosh toward me and away, his eyes sealed shut, dark lashes fanned out like wild plumage. I turn on *Sesame Street* and KJ plunks down in his plush Elmo chair. His little fingers drill into a plastic tube of candy and pluck out rainbow-colored morsels — red, blue and yellow. He is agile this way, the MacGyver of candy extraction. It seems like a good time to wash dishes, so I go into the kitchen and run the hot water, drizzle the soap in the sink. The crusty cups, bowls and plates disappear beneath the dancing suds. I let my hands swim, explore the smooth lip of a coffee cup and the sharp prong of each fork. I stretch my fingers out like starfish and feel the water gush around them, warm and fragrant. This is my spa. On the television, Elmo is squealing to his goldfish, Dorothy, but I manage to shrink his voice as I squeeze my eyes shut. I'm standing on the ugly linoleum in my puke-stained bathrobe with my hands in the kitchen sink, but it could be the rim of a mountain, a golden beach on an island or the little pond where Emmet splashed. I can go anywhere in my mind. Imagination has always rescued me.

When the water begins to cool, KJ scuttles in behind me and jolts me out of my thoughts. I reach for a towel to dry my hands and knock my hip into the open silverware drawer. *Why is the silverware drawer open?* I find out when the baby lets out a shriek and I run to the living room. The swing has stopped moving and KJ is leaning over the baby, his little hand poised to groom his brother, but not with a hairbrush. He's holding a utensil he swiped from the kitchen — a steak knife. The baby's face is twisted and red, and KJ is closing in with a stainless-steel blade aimed at a silken crest of hair. I am afraid to scream so I hold my breath instead. I tip forward like a wind-blown tree and gingerly snatch the knife with one quick motion. I stand frozen, gripping the blade until my breath returns. The room pulsates as I gulp down air and then exhale. My heart begins to beat again.

When Saturday comes, I shop for baby carriers and find a navy canvas jobber with adjustable straps and a cute galactic pattern. From now on, I will keep Sym strapped to me like a new body part.

***

In the early mornings, the sun sifts through the blinds and we lie in bed, feeding. My postpartum body is like Play-Doh, shaped anew by a flux of hormones. I am alternately sweaty and chilled as if ice courses through my veins. Baby's mouth is a thirsty waterhole and I watch his lips pucker and suck, pucker and suck with fervor. He sinks into the crook of my arm and I conjure the way it felt with KJ. Everything is different: my body, his whimper, our bond. I look into his eyes and I see new territory. The bulk of him, the hungry animal mouth of him.

I recall hearing mothers saying they love all their children the same. The phrase flits about in my consciousness. What does it mean? "Same," as in equal measure? How can a mother pour her love into each child-vessel in precise doses? What happens if one child cracks and needs more love — more time, more patience, more care? I shut my eyes and feel the sticky sheets close over me like a licked envelope. No doubt I love this heaving, suckling lump. But my instincts say there is nothing "same" about him.

Symeon: 7 pounds, 14 ounces, 21 inches long.

***

Her office is sunny and comfortable, the right size for a two-way chat. I drop into a plush leather sofa. I'm hers for an hour. She sits in front of a window and I watch the light twinkle on her shoulders. She's middle-aged, blonde, smart and kind. I am exhausted and I don't know if I've even brushed my hair.

"Chronic migraines, but it's more than that," I hear myself say when she asks what's brought me in. "I feel like I just don't care."

Her eyebrows sweep together, and she leans in. "Care?"

"About keeping it together anymore — going to work, even brushing my hair," I say. One hand rakes through a nap of curls. As we talk, I discover a tiny hole in my pants, just above the knee. *You poor slob*, I might have thought on another day. But today, I don't think. I don't cross my leg to hide my peeping flesh. I openly tug at the fabric and wriggle my fingernail into the spot. I explain that J is a Jekyll and Hyde, that he alternately loves and hates me, and I can't crack this code. He disappears for hours, sometimes a full day. He takes the car we share and leaves me panicked when we're out of diapers. Desperate when we're out of milk.

"I got a goddamn haircut," he tells me. "I went to the mall." Doors slam and I just want the noise to stop. I am numb, anesthetized by the sound of crying babies, my husband's anger, and chores, chores, chores.

Paresthesia is prolonged pressure that puts a limb to sleep, constricts the blood flow. I am a hobbling mama-limb, dead inside. I operate on autopilot. The fact that I made it into this office surprises me. It started with a flier, an employee resource letter with a list of phone numbers and corporate wellness tools. Three free counseling sessions for anyone feeling overwhelmed. That's me, I thought. And I knew I had to come because my boys need me whole. They deserve more than this sloppy, unfeeling woman I've become. I fear for them because I don't know who I might be if given more time to unravel from myself. Last week I missed three days of work because I couldn't muster the strength to slide both feet into my shoes.

As I sit in her office plucking at my pant leg, I don't recall dialing the number, making the appointment, driving to her office. She asks me probing questions, about my childhood, my marriage, my babies, my job. I state everything as fact. There's no emotion in my voice, no tears shaking my words. I wonder if she thinks I'm composed or psychotic. Am I?

"How do I get through this?" I ask when we are nearing the one-hour mark. The room is dense with my stories, pieces of me broken off like the hard bits of a cracked nut she's been shelling.

"Get back to writing," she replies.

I don't remember telling her what it meant to put pen to paper, but I must have expressed it somehow. Maybe I told her about poetry, about my favorite authors and the journals I used to keep.

On my way home, I stop and buy a hardcover journal. The next day, I find myself writing as the sun comes up, and it's like crying through my fingers. But at least I can feel again.

Chapter 5

Grandma

I was sipping lukewarm coffee near a window when Grandma died. What I learned was painful but not profound — the world keeps spinning. When loss crashes in, it spins ad nauseam.

Her death did not surprise us. Age had eroded her slowly, the way a hillside crumbles over time, each year chipping away the soil of her strength, the clay of her memory. I was ten years old when I realized Grandma would not live forever. The sight of her poking an insulin syringe in her belly pricked me to the core. When the doctor gave her a bulky metal walker to use, I feigned excitement, hopping on the bars as if it were playground equipment. But at night, I cried when I thought about what it meant.

Our connection had solidified in my infancy. I was a shrieking, inconsolable savage — the sort of baby women heard about while being warned about the pitfalls of motherhood. Frazzled and worn thin, as if sandpapered by the tasks of parenting, my mother walked me down the street to Grandma's house. I seemed to know even then how well I fit in her arms and how much we belonged together. I spent most of my time at her side, where a simple magic floated between us. When I was a child, we watched murder mysteries on television, discussed the books I was reading (books she had also read in her youth) and listened to the squabbling birds in the pine trees that towered outside her little white house on 66th street.

She told me I was one of her favorite people, that I was smart and sensitive, her little Rica Tula. But of all the gifts she gave me, the gem of literature shines brightest in my memory. Inside the bubble of our days, the swirl of Grandma's lilac perfume and the fairy dust of her fables drew me to her on the sofa. Tugging a curl from my head, she would examine the strand in her hand and recite a Longfellow poem:

> *There was a little girl,*
> *Who had a little curl,*
> *Right in the middle of her forehead.*
> *When she was good,*
> *She was very good indeed,*
> *But when she was bad she was horrid.*

Then we'd read the cracked leather book she had saved from her youth, a small trove of rhythmic treasures. She'd remember those poems, even after she had forgotten my name. And I would remember the rhyme she wrote — the lines that broke my heart.

"Write me something," I had begged. I wrote my own poem and presented it to her, my child-hand clutching the ribbon-tied ends of my masterpiece. The next day, she called me to recite her work:

The days are short.
The nights are long.
Soon I'll hear old winter's song.
Tell me please,
How can it be…
I've grown so old,
So suddenly.

"It's not particularly eloquent," she said. But I began to understand the brevity of life and the way time seems to speed up in one's later years, leaving its passengers careening frighteningly forward.

***

In my teen years, Grandma pressed a wad of stiff bills into my hand, her non-negotiable reward for the dye jobs I did on her hair — summer blond. She grew up in a well-to-do-household. They were the kind of family that knew which fork to use and why. But she married my poor grandfather anyway, and never looked back. Still, her impeccable grooming always stuck, and it made me think she was celebrating life at all times — even the mundane moments. She would dress up to fetch the mail because that was reason enough for red lipstick. I massaged her scalp with shampoo over the kitchen sink and rinsed away the store-bought dye. At barely five-feet tall, she had to stand on a small, plastic stool so I could do the work efficiently. When we finished, I would twist the damp strands in a towel and walk her into the bathroom for the next phase of blow-drying and styling. She was wobbly by then, well into her 70s and with a few surgeries and heart attacks behind her. Her memory was fickle, coming in and out of frequency like an old television set with rabbit ear antennas. Some days I sat with her and chatted. After short periods of silence, she turned to me and said, "Hello dear. When did you come in?"

Those were the first murky steps toward the slope, and I had the feeling a part of me was breaking away, like a branch snapping off during a storm.

***

After Sym was born, I learned the nursing home was hiring and Grandma needed me. If I could do the clinical work and pass the state test, the education was free and I had a job. I got a note from my doctor six weeks post-delivery, and I started my training.

The place smelled of bleach and urine. It reminded me of the word *pungent*, which Grandma taught me when I was a child asking how I might describe the smell of a pickle. The linoleum floors were waxed to perfection, as if a bit of shine could offset the melancholy. When I saw Grandma slumped in her wheelchair in the shared room, it was as though I was looking at somebody else's grandmother — some gray and forlorn woman. No more summer blonde or red lipstick. No more perfume or songs. I sat down and did the only thing that felt safe in that moment — I read. At first, it was the newspaper, which was always available on her nightstand. But on other visits, I read poetry from the books I'd found at a used bookstore that carried tattered volumes of the classics. She read with me, mouthing the words in a small, stranger's voice. Her inflection never faltered, and it was the only way I could tell that Grandma was inside there somewhere, like a stone at the bottom of a well.

I worked the night shift and got used to the odors and the nonstop blinking and buzzing of call lights — a chaos like rush hour traffic. After my shifts, I crept into Grandma's room, leaned over her sleeping body and tucked the blankets beneath her chin as if to repay the favors of my youth. One morning, her eyes flashed open and she shrieked at the sight of me, a stranger in her slow-fading universe.

"Get out," she hollered. Devastated, I ran from the room, straight through the sliding glass doors and into the dark wet parking lot. I stood there and let the rain pelt me until my clothes were heavy and my hair was slicked against my neck. The next day, I made a transfer to another unit.

On the day Grandma died, my aunt called with the news. It was as though a song of 80 plus years had abruptly stopped playing — the cadence of her breath, the tempo of her heartbeat. But the orchestra of life droned on.

I could not attend her funeral. I didn't need to see Grandma's decked out bones, boxed up like department store shoes. I held her where I needed her — in the place she held me best: on that sofa near the window in her house, where the sun spun gold and nothing seemed impossible.

***

I groped for meaning after Grandma died. At night, I'd watch the moonlight spilling into the room and feel the weight of the day on my chest. "Breathe," I'd tell my lungs. That's when I started to pray.

At first, I didn't understand it, didn't know to whom I was praying or whether I was doing it right. Fold your hands? Kneel in the dark? Cross-legged, head bowed?

I thought about what I'd learned at youth services on Wednesday nights when Mom took turns carpooling with the neighbors. She watched *Miami Vice* at home while my siblings and I ran relay races in the gymnasium and sang songs at St. John's during Awana services. A Christian group, Awana kids wore vests and accrued patches for reciting scriptures and doing good deeds. Having been churched throughout her child-hood, Mom wanted to give us the gift of God without crack-ing a Bible or sitting on a pew. But religion remained a distant cousin for me, an entity outside of the household. I only prayed sporadically and without much intent. But now I longed for certainties, for the grace and assurances I lacked in real life.

It wasn't just Grandma's death that piqued my interest in religion. Life felt especially flimsy. My marriage was falling apart, and crime was ramping up in my neighborhood. A strange man chased me from my car to my doorstep on a sticky night in July, then someone tossed a brick through my windshield. This was life, rife with death, failing marriages and flying bricks. Who was going to keep us safe? When a coworker at the nursing home invited me to her church, I bought a massive leather-bound Bible with gold gilded pages. Heavy as an anchor, it was the kind of book I hoped could keep a family grounded. With J off at work, I dressed the boys in collared shirts and slicked back the tufts of their wild hair. We drove twenty miles or so to the little brick church on a rural road, beside sagging barns and rusted-out Fords. It was midwinter in Wisconsin and the air was frigid and opaque.

The parking lot was crammed with cars when I arrived 10 minutes late. I found a spot in the back and we sloshed toward the double doors, icy puddles breaking loose beneath our church shoes. A woman greeted us and handed me a pam-phlet. Music rose up from the sanctuary, a halo of delicate hymns. We ducked inside behind the crowd and found seats near the back, a place where I could dip one toe in the action but remain close to the door. If the boys decided to fight, scream, or pick their noses bloody, I could scoop them up and make a quick exit.

Thirty minutes in, I felt light, like a cotton dress on a clothesline in the sun. But then, as if all of heaven had punked me, I spotted KJ. He'd slipped out of his seat and onto the carpet. I watched his little fingers work and realized he was no longer playing with the Matchbox cars he'd shoved in his pockets that morning. He looked up at me, face awash with mischief. He'd successfully tied a woman's sneakers together. Shoe to shoe, via the bunny-ears method. The woman stood up and pointed a long, angry finger across the pew. "Look what he did," she said, gesturing toward her knotted-up sneakers, my wayward kid and me.

Looking back now, I feel empathy for that woman who made such a fuss about child's play. As I recall, she was alone that day and had probably come in floundering, just as I had. But when she aimed her finger at me, it might as well have been a gun, and I didn't have the capacity to feel anything other than shame. I don't recall how, but I had punished my son and it must have been severe because his reaction is seared in my memory — his contorted little face, swollen with remorse. When a child looks at his mother that way, something inside her cracks open. Like a broken tooth exposed to the air, her whole soul begins to ache.

Years later, I'd read another mother's version, which only compounded the ache.

"It's so awful, attacking your child. It's the worst thing I know, to shout loudly at this 50-pound being with his huge, trusting brown eyes. It's like bitch-slapping E.T.," wrote Anne Lamott in her book, *Traveling Mercies*.

That night I went home disappointed, feeling as though religion were a club from which I'd been rejected. But at some point, there was a quiet snippet of time in which I found myself in the bathtub, bubbles shimmering and popping against my skin. I felt my whole body begin to tremble from my core.

Before I knew what was happening, I was crying a deep, guttural cry. The kind of cry that comes after a death or a crisis. A nose-draining, stars-seeing kind of cry. It came from somewhere so deep within, my own tears seemed strange to me. And I felt something else there with me: the presence of love, fierce and enveloping like the pull of a hug. God, is that you?

**

We attended more church services, first sporadically, then every Sunday. I had to ease my boys into the habit. And still there were days when Sym would cry too hard and too long in the little basement nursery. Another mother would yank me out of the service and I'd retrieve him, red-faced and gasping. It was always so much work to get there: the endless buttons and zippers and tussling with hair. Then there were shoes and laces, car seats and heated negotiations about which superheroes could attend the service and why we would not be wearing capes. The whole ordeal was actually church foreplay because by the time we pulled in the lot, the three of us needed heavy doses of prayer and forgiveness. Being called to the nursery was yet another obstacle. I'd hoist Sym up and jiggle him down the polished marble floors outside of the sanctuary, his dense body like a boulder on my hip. But we'd continue our jostling in the large, empty hall and slowly, his head would ease onto my shoulder and he'd sink his weary self into me. My heart would stop its rapid thump and his breath would stroke my neck like warm feathers. There in the church, my feet moved across the marble until there was only the force of my steps to keep us afloat in the room.

I think back now and I yearn for that little boy, wish I could hold him again. How many times since then have I wanted him to sink himself into me that way? To lean on me and just shut his eyes? But in those days, all I could feel was his weight in my arms. All I could wish for was relief, for someone to hold me instead.

With Sym on my hip and KJ happy in the children's group, I'd slip back into the service and find a lonesome pew. I'd settle Sym on my lap and sit, jittery and ready to bolt at the first sign of trouble, staring at the back of his head as if sending him telepathic messages. *Please, little volcano, don't erupt.*

Eventually, we all got the hang of church and started showing up for Wednesday evening sermons too when only retirees and hungry newcomers made the trip. So often I heard mothers say, "Parenting doesn't come with a handbook," when faced with a dilemma, but in my mind, this was the instruction manual. Here was the teacher — standing behind the lectern, gray-haired and offering the weekly word.

At home, J became angrier and more distant while I inched closer to religion as if it were an alternate lover, a genuine companion. On nights when the bed felt too big and my husband chose the upstairs sofa and ESPN over me, I snuggled up with the Psalms, relieved rather than disappointed. Dreamy-eyed like a teen who'd been slipped a love note in science class, I clung to the primitive poetry. And I didn't feel alone anymore. When I picked up my Bible, a conversation occurred, and I felt there was someone there listening. Always listening. Suddenly, the religious nonsense seemed practical, wise even. In the quiet mornings with a mug of coffee at my side and the sun creeping out of the night sky, I could hear my grandma's long-gone voice echoing in my head, "I don't know what I'd do without my Bible." I remember the confusion I felt when she'd said that many years prior. But as a young girl, I'd tucked the phrase in the attic of my mind, treating it like a pair of special shoes I'd need for a certain kind of path. I was on that path now, unpacking those shoes, her words. At last, I understood them.

My boys understood too. As much as little boys could. They seemed to absorb my faith as if by osmosis. Seeing me near the window, face alight with sun and prayer, KJ entered the room one morning in his Spiderman pajamas. Our eyes met and his face became urgent — my perceptive, loving, first-born child.

"No, Sym," he hollered at his brother who was two steps behind, holding an armful of toys. "Mom's in a meeting with God."

And just like that, they left me to it.

***

New friends were hard to make because no one my age was married or had started a family just yet. None had diaper bags to pack, boogers to chisel off the bedroom wall. It was easy for me to become a groupie. Whereas before my church days, Christian rock was an oxymoron, I began experimenting with new bands, scouring music stores and amassing a collection of music that made me feel buoyant. Some nights I'd look around at the shitty apartment we were renting, the dark-paneled walls, the antiquated linoleum, the musty basement aura. A spider's web of a place. I'd turn on a song and my friends would float in. Not actual friends, but my band friends, the artists whose music I played. They were as real as any people in my life. And I could commiserate with them because they knew about the loneliness I felt, the animal inside me that sharpened its teeth on my pain. These people sang songs about their desires to be understood, loved unconditionally, nurtured and cared for. And they knew about brokenness, loss, disappointment and suffering. They were strong, resilient, fueled by a life of faith. Even so, they longed to be held just as I did. I wanted everything they wanted and had. As the music filled the room, I heard my own voice in the lyrics. It was as though the dark panels parted and everything — the basement funk, my nagging insecurities and general misery was eclipsed by some kind of temporary bliss. The rhythm shook the room and all the broken parts of me reassembled to form a choir and sing. I sang with the windows open and the summer air pushing in; the boys giggled and hopped up beside me. I sang, "He loves us, oh how he loves us." And somehow it made it okay that my husband didn't — not so much anymore. I sang until the ache lifted, the room shifted, the light entered and I collapsed onto the floor. Weightless.

***

I learn to listen for the rumblings that signal an earthquake. I breathe deeply in the moments, days or weeks between my husband's outbursts. Still, he occasionally takes me by surprise as dark moods rear up like Dobermans behind a fence. I hear the front door open and our boys tromp inside.

"Dad took us to the park, Mom," KJ exclaims. His jeans are grass-stained at the knees and he wears little crusts of leaves in his hair.

"I see that," I say, examining his hands for dirt.

"Wash your hands, boys," J says before I can utter my directive. He's quick to cut me off at the pass, to assert the rules so I don't have to. In those days I see this as good-dad behavior, authoritative and helpful. But looking back I wonder if it was his way of diminishing me.

In the kitchen, I slice warm banana bread and pile the crumbling pieces on plates.

"I made you a snack," I sing-say, and the boys barrel into the kitchen with wet hands dripping at their sides.

"I was just going to take a bath..." I start to tell J who suddenly appears in the doorway. He is holding the remote-control Hummer he bought for Sym last week, a chunky orange truck that cost way too much for a toddler.

"What the fuck is this?" he asks, pointing to the truck's bent antenna, which bobs up and down in his hand.

I can't speak. My mouth is slack, and I've forgotten how to operate my face. "I told you not to let him play with this, didn't I?" he hollers. His eyes are hard as onyx.

"He begged," I start to say, but my husband interjects...

"He's not old enough for this yet and now it's ruined."

I want to tell him that it is cruel to buy a child a toy he can't play with and it was stupid to spend our money that way, but I know better than to say these things to that face — the dark face.

He tosses the toy on the floor and I fix my eyes on it. They are pinned to its rubber wheels as it bounces on the linoleum. I hear the car keys jingle and I look up as J exits the kitchen. I stand there immobilized, caught in the shadow of his anger.

The front door slams.

Thanksgiving Day follows, and although we have plans, there's no sign of J. I'm too embarrassed to tell his sister what's happened, so I say someone is sick and it may be contagious. "Sorry, we can't make it this time." Then I open the fridge and remember how I put off the shopping this week, thinking we'd be feasting today. I order a crappy pizza for the boys and me. I plop it on the table and the three of us lean over the box, pull out greasy slices and let the cheese stretch out on our chins. There's no laughter or chatter, only three hungry mouths chewing as we listen for the sound of the door.

***

A few weeks pass and a new tenant moves in upstairs. A young, single mom, who throws wild parties on the weekends.

It's none of my business, except that she sleeps late and I find her son in a sagging diaper, crying in the hall near my door.

"My mom said we should play for a while," her 7-year-old daughter explains. "I babysit, sometimes," she says proudly, as her brother wriggles off her hip and slides down her flannel-clad leg. It is almost noon and she is still wearing her pajamas.

"Don't you want to get dressed?" I ask.

"My mom locked the door because she's sleeping," she says. She smiles as if honored by this, deemed grown up enough to be fending for herself in the world.

I pause for a moment and then say, "Come inside." I don't know what else to do, so I pour Froot Loops into plastic bowls in the kitchen and let them stay awhile.

"Can you believe her?" I say to J at dinner. I'm rehashing my day while winding my fork around a pile of pasta. "I spent 5 hours with her kids today and she didn't even show up to ask where they were."

His eyes sharpen. He drops his fork and it makes a loud, tinging sound on the edge of his plate. He leans across the table as if to tell me something I should write down. It comes out in a spit-growl.

"Don't be so goddamn judgmental."

My heart swings like a pendulum. Fear. Love. Fear. Love. Fear.

The next party is especially rowdy, and I'm gearing up for a 16-hour shift at work. In three hours my 5 a.m. alarm will sound and the music from upstairs is pulsating. I have beaten my pillow into a lump, so I get up and find my husband lying on the floor in the living room, watching a movie in the dark.

"If you don't go up there and ask her to turn down her music, I'm calling the police to break up her party," I say.

J adjusts himself, shifting the pillows beneath his head on the floor. He does not look up at me.

"Mind your own damn business," he sneers, pointing the remote at the television and raising the volume to 30. He begins calling me names, muttering under his breath. A lava-like heat simmers at my core, threatening to engulf me. I'm tired. Physically, mentally, emotionally. I have reached my limit, with him, with our neighbor, with everything. We are one word away from collapse. And then he says it — "Bitch." It explodes in the room like gunfire and a woman I don't recognize appears. She hovers above my husband who lies numbly on the floor. She reaches down and her hands look like mine. She slaps his face once, twice, and again. She pulls back a foot and thrusts it into his side. She is ominous, dangerous, hot-faced and tear-stained. Her angry curls thrash in the blue-green glow of the television.

"Asshole," she screams above the sound of the blaring movie and the thumping party overhead.

The man is covering his head with his pillow. And suddenly, she stops, as if her battery has died.

I realize she is me and I am her — a woman with another face.

***

After my violent outburst, I meet with a church counselor and tell him my story through tears. I cannot look him in the eye, so I focus instead on the ragged wad of tissue in my lap.

He clears his throat and responds, "Let us trust God to restore your broken marriage." He rests a warm hand on my shoulder and I drink in his words, swallowing the message like a patient swigging medicine. Later, I will look back and realize it was poison.

Chapter 6

A Bookmark in a Horror Story

We are homeowners now. We have moved from our rented duplex into the two-story bungalow we bought. It was J's idea. And although I'm nervous about money and the shifting ground of my marriage, I'm also thrilled to have something that feels permanent. Could brick and mortar be our Band-aid?

Our sons have a large playroom with its own little bathroom, the entire upstairs, the perfect space for sword fights and wrestling matches. A skylight tilts its golden eye upward, and I think I'd like to be the child in this playroom, lying on my back and looking up and out.

Upon moving in, J bought a gigantic electronic racetrack and clicked each piece together, showing the boys how to make their cars zoom along the superspeedway. Cartoons, pirate movies and video games rumble the playroom walls at high volume, and I can't decide who's having more fun: J or the boys.

Downstairs, I've painted and stenciled wooden furniture with rosebuds and soft ivy vines.

"Well, look at Martha Stewart," J says, examining my work. He scoops up our son and asks, "Who wants trouble?"

This is their game — one of many that begin with a challenge and end with a scramble on the carpet and a pile of bodies sprawled out. They giggle and gasp, look genuinely pleased with themselves. I watch my little boys watch their dad, their faces aflame with excitement. He's hunched over, palms and knees on the floor, a jungle-gym-dad in waiting. They lasso their bony arms around his waist and neck and hop on for a ride across the room. I smile, grateful in these instances for the man-child I married. As they tussle and yelp like off-leash dogs, I stack dishes in the cabinets and consider what to make for dinner.

As Christmas approaches, I work double shifts at the hospital, and J works more hours too. Many nights, he creeps in well past midnight, rarely sleeping in our bedroom. He opts for the sofa instead. But for all the hours he puts in, I never see his paychecks. Occasionally, he announces he'll be short on his share of the bills.

"You'll have to cover the rest," he says. I start to protest, to slam a cupboard, pitch a fit, but he lobs a warning at me with dark brows raised like a pair of swords. I have learned to pick my battles.

One afternoon, I think about calling his work to check up on him. I can't think of an excuse to speak with him and he's already explained why I shouldn't call: He's working with machines and chemicals in a busy, noisy plant. It's not the kind of place where you can grab a phone and chat. Still, I hear a voice prodding me. I consider it as I shimmy my arms into my coat and step out onto the front porch. The wind rakes a cool hand through my hair as I walk down the street toward KJ's school. I stop at the corner, let the traffic pass, watch the long yellow buses assemble. I'm dialing the numbers in my mind. I see my fingers pressing the buttons on the phone in my head. *It's just a phone call,* I tell myself. *I'll just call my husband. Wives call husbands all the time.* But my hands are shaking, and I realize I'm holding my breath. I stop walking, look around, listen as the doors swish open on the bus and kids whirl around me on the sidewalk. I find a spot near the school entrance, a place where I can lean against the cold brick and steady my thinking.

I feel it. Truth is pursuing me. It rattles the windows of our home. I sense its presence now and in the silent hours when I am alone. When J is gone and I doubt he's really at work. It ticks like a clock, persistent and taunting. But truth can be subtle enough to dismiss. I realize I have to be ready to face it. Facts don't have power without belief, without action. But accepting facts can change a woman's heart, can change a family's future. I am not ready for change. I want nothing more than to cling to the family I invented in my mind. I want to live in the bliss of ignorance, in the blur of a world where I can be both married and happy. But on some level, I already know this is an impossibility. It's only a matter of time before the truth of us demands to be seen and dealt with.

When KJ comes bouncing in my direction, we head home for little bowls of pretzels and cups of juice. All the while, I'm plotting the call I know I must make, and the more I think about it, the angrier I get. *This should not be such a big deal. A wife should be able to call her husband.* I'm standing near the sink when a surge of indignation sends me to the phone. I dial with a steady hand and then ask a man politely for my husband. In a hoarse voice, he says, "J doesn't work today, ma'am." I hear the churning of machines in the background. The churning in my mind. The man hangs up. I feel the weight of the phone in my hand.

It's late and the boys are already in bed when J comes home smelling like expensive cologne. We sit down together for a meal and I don't remember bringing it up, don't recall what I say as I am balancing the food on my fork. But somehow, between fork lifting and drink sipping, I weave in the information about my phone call. His reaction is everything I thought it would be. He pulls back from the table and his chair squeals across the kitchen floor.

"Do you want to get me fired for taking personal calls?"

This is not a question.

He stands up so hard, his chair tips back and wobbles on two legs. Sound swims away from my ears and the room becomes a vibration, a slow-motion scene in which a girl awaits her fate. I can feel his rage against my skin, cold and sharp like a knife pressed to my throat. He storms away and I sit alone at the table — silent.

A few weeks later, I am attempting to pack J a sandwich when I find a pair of pink satin panties in his lunch box. Fishing them out with two leery fingers, I hold them up and ask, "What the hell is this?"

He looks directly at me. "Must be a prank," he says. "You don't know the kind of guys I work with."

I throw his lunch box on the counter and it lands with a clunk.

"Bullshit," is all I can muster before his face begins to morph. Eyes like ammunition.

He takes two steps toward me and leans in. I'm pressed between him and the wall, a bookmark in a horror story. "You have some serious jealousy issues," he says, spitting each syllable at my face.

Again, I am silent. I'll never get a straight answer from a crooked man.

***

We all pile into our Chevy Malibu and I balance a hot tray of cocktail wieners on my lap.

"You're too damn handsome," J hollers to the boys as they scramble to find their seatbelts. He leans into the backseat with his eyes narrowed in their direction. "Who told you to look so damn handsome today? So. Damn. Handsome! We're going to church, not Hollywood," he says.

He begins jabbing the boys with his finger and they curl up and giggle. Their little feet thrash in the backseat and I shove the wieners aside so I can grab Sym's untied shoelace and fasten a quick bow.

At the potluck, we are happily married like everyone else, and J mingles with the crowds while he approaches the line for more lemonade. I watch Pastor John shake his hand then they stand together for a moment and chat, occasionally chuckling or nodding in mutual agreement. My husband is pleasant today. He is the charismatic man who slid his phone number across the counter at a Milwaukee gas station. I am on the other side of the church gymnasium, fielding basketballs and other playground equipment. The boys are sweaty, and they scamper around like baby squirrels. Sym found a jump rope and KJ is busy with two boys and a football. Their little tanks are full of lemonade and apple pie, and they could go for miles. I look up and see J returning with a small plate and a plastic cup. "I brought you a piece of cheesecake," he says. "With strawberries."

We go home happy until gravity takes hold and pushes us back to ourselves, J on the upstairs sofa and me with my face in a book. After work, he stays out late and when I ask, he says, "sports." He likes to watch races, basketball, football and all the rest on the big screens downtown with a basket of chicken wings and a side of ranch. This goes on for months and I'm alternately angry and relieved. Angry because this is no marriage. Relieved because the boys are in bed and Lucy and Ethel are on TV. In the quiet house, I can spread out in front of old sitcoms and laugh. I can read books about other families and forget everything I know about my own.

***

Six months pass before J is in the mood for another church function. And really, he's not even in the mood. But I have somehow convinced him to attend. *This is our ticket,* I think. *Can't God save us?*

J dresses quietly, slowly. I try to watch the clock without watching the clock. When he turns his back, I steal a glance and sigh. *Maybe, if traffic is good,* I think. But he lumbers about, opening dresser drawers and slamming them until he finds his belt and slowly begins threading it through the loops on his pants. Five more minutes. *Maybe if traffic is really good and we get a great parking spot and there's a pew way in back...* The boys are on the stairs, tossing toy cars down and declaring winners. "Can I watch cartoons now?" KJ calls out, bored with his game.

"We're going to church," I say.

"But when? What's taking so long?" he bellows.

"Shut your mouth, son." J snaps. Then, "Please," like bad punctuation.

The boys and I collectively harden, frozen until J grabs the car keys and they clink us to life once again. We are off to church.

When we arrive, the congregation is on its feet and music fills the room. I weave through the center aisle with the boys at my side. Perfume wafts from every direction and people smile tiny, distracted smiles as we scout for seats. When I find a pew, I hunker down with the boys and search the room for J. *Where is J?* There are little old ladies clutching their adult grandsons and young women corralling their children. A pig-tailed girl stands in her seat and yanks at her father's elbow. He scoops her into his lap. The ushers are shutting the big oak doors and as they thud to a close, I see J through the glass pane. His black hair glistens in the sun-dappled hall. I watch as he makes his way toward the foyer and then disappears. Someone picks him up and I don't know how it goes down, only that he doesn't reappear until well after midnight.

He's silent the next day, so I decide to make some noise. I don't know where to begin with my words, so I let the draw-ers do the talking. Slam. Slam. Slam. Our entire house is indig-nant on my behalf. When I search the cupboards for a pot, I clang the cookware together like cymbals, again and again and again. When I find my pot, I place it on the stove and let it crash down so hard the boys turn to see what's happened. Then I hustle out of the kitchen because the bathrooms need a good cleaning. I am hurricane-wife.

The real storm hits a few nights later. The snow comes down in a hectic, bleach-white haze and I watch it cling to the trees outside. J's words come slow like syrup from the bottom of a bottle. After hours of silence, he finally says, "I want a divorce." Before I can feel the impact of his statement, KJ runs in from the playroom.

"Dad, come see the fort we built," he pleads, yanking J's arm.

"In a minute, son," he says in a voice that's almost a whis-per. KJ bobs out of the room and we begin to argue. This is the end of us, and I feel like the little girl on the cracked ce-ment step.

"What about the mortgage? The boys' schools? Their playroom — their neighborhood friends? We have everything here," I say. But I know it's a lie. I am the girl who believes every lie, even my own.

I keep talking, cobbling together lists like a salesperson trying to close the deal. "We're so close to the library and my work, and maybe if you went to church with us…" My voice trails off. We're quiet for a moment then J speaks again.

"Would you even be with me if it weren't for the boys?" It's the first time he has looked at me today and suddenly, I wish he wouldn't. His eyes are sad. So sad. Broken window eyes.

I know the words he wants to hear, the assurance he gropes for even as the truth has returned to rattle our walls. My answer is small but mighty, an arrow in the bow of my mouth. Once I say it, I know I can't stop its trajectory. But neither can I lie.

"No."

I watch him leave the room. It seems we don't talk about divorce again. We just do it.

***

My sister announces she found our cousin, who led her to our dad. He reappears in my life with grand tales that only partially explain his absence. When I see him, I stand awkwardly in my sister's kitchen, unsure of my hands, my smile, the rules that apply in this scenario. But he is confident, and he hugs me as if he knows me. I wonder if he does, if it's possible that he could have carried me with him all these years. "I would recognize you anywhere," he says. I watch his hands move to the beat of his words, slender hands like my brother's. He tells me he wrote poems in jail. Poems like I write — me, his daughter. I am someone's daughter. He is brown-skinned and blue-jeaned and familiar as if from a dream. He is deja vu.

I think of the metal box I found in the hall closet when I was 15. The crusty pages of court documents, the sight of his name — the name of my dad. I think of the days I dreamed I

49

could find him, the bus fare that jingled in my pocket. *I could ride the bus straight to him.* Which bus would take me there?

Now he promises to treat us to ice cream and shopping — father, daughter, grandsons. We wait for him on a Sunday afternoon. The boys place their plastic army men in tidy rows near my feet. I sit cross-legged, watching the street, waiting for my father to arrive. Waiting, waiting. The weather is turning, and the colors make me hopeful. A kaleidoscope of leaves is splayed across the grass: orange, red, yellow — the jewels of autumn. When KJ asks if it's time to go yet, I check my watch and realize how late it's gotten. *How did it get so late?*

"Let's go inside, guys," I say.

I hear the ghost of my mother's voice whispering in my head — my father is worthless.

***

Two weeks post-divorce I am back at the house that is no longer my house.

J decided to keep it, although I can't fathom how he will pay the mortgage. But it's not my problem anymore. I have taken what was mine: vases and valances, little lamps that lit the corners of our rooms and the trinkets I hoped could make a home. I found a place for everything in an apartment across town, and it fits but it doesn't.

The wind has pitched the porch chairs on their sides, and I stand at my old door, resisting the urge to straighten them. The grass is long and weedy, and the plants I left are now prickly brown shoots, potted ugly afters. Before I can knock or think about whether I should knock, J opens the door. He smells like Drakkar Noir and the memories come flooding back. I picture him standing in the bedroom we shared, wet from a shower, spritzing this man-scent on his chest. "Who wants some smell good," he'd ask, and the boys would line up, lift their shirts and giggle as he sprayed their little bodies.

"The boys are upstairs watching a movie," he says.

I glance down at my feet, considering my options.

"Do you want to come in and wait?" he asks, stepping aside so I can enter.

I don't answer but I follow him into the house where cozy rugs once warmed my feet and the aroma of a meal in the oven filled every room. Now there are pizza crusts in open boxes, Mountain Dew bottles, crumpled receipts and stacks of old mail. In the sink, there are no dishes. Probably because there are no dishes. Neither is there any furniture. The house is a dorm room on steroids. And when I excuse myself to the bathroom, there is no toilet paper on the roll. Instead, a pile of Burger King napkins.

Because there's nowhere to sit, I lie on the floor in the living room downstairs and listen as the boys' movie shakes the walls in the upstairs playroom. J finds a spot next to me and we begin to chat. It's like we are relearning each other, and ourselves too. I am someone else now, no longer his wife. When he looks at me, he looks *at* me and not through me, the way you look at a person you just met when you're attempting to know who they are. This is new territory and I am a new woman, someone he deems worthy of manners. His movements are cautious, his eyes quizzical. I can tell he's noticing things about me as he explores the landscape of my face. When we were married, he filled out an insurance questionnaire and his answers surprised me.

"You've got me down as 5'7" and 110 pounds," I said. "I'm 5'2" and 125 pounds. Do you even know my eye color?"

If he had to fill out that form today, I wonder what he would write.

We get quiet and I feel his hand edge toward mine on the carpet. It's inches away, idling like an engine. He's so close I can feel his breath, but I am lost in the shadows on the ceiling. Shadows everywhere.

"I made a big mistake," he says in a whisper that could be a roar.

I swallow the shockwave in the room and say, "I can't fix this."

Chapter 7

ADHD

Things get better and worse, better and worse. Our apartment is in a quiet building with a manicured lawn where the boys pound snow into their gloves and launch ice bombs in the yard. In the summer, they meander with stick swords, poke beetles and collect dandelions in their muddy fists.

"Look, Mom, we brought you flowers."

On good days I serve chocolate cake at the kitchen counter and fill their cups with cold milk. On bad days, Sym yanks the television to the floor or gut-punches me in the grocery store checkout line.

A year prior, during Sym's first week of preschool, the teacher had pulled me into the classroom. A plump young woman, her rosy cheeks had gone pale. We stood for an awkward second as I considered taking a seat on one of the miniature chairs.

"We've had some problems," she began.

Between story hour and snack time, my 40-pound son had flipped over a table and knocked a bookshelf to the ground.

A heap of hardcover books bore witness as she pointed and cleared her throat. It was the first of many classroom outbursts I would hear about from every teacher, counselor, or faculty member I met in a cold conference room or office. And she was the first of many who summed it up in four letters: ADHD. The symptoms: impulsivity, anger, hyperactivity. Check, check and check. I had to admit he fit the profile. So I went home and typed the letters into the search bar, then chased them down the internet rabbit hole.

Was this a marketing ploy to peddle a high-priced drug? *My son is willful, spirited, shaken by the family drama.* But then I would watch him with KJ, two brothers so vastly different — one child captivated by the cartoons, the other rocking wildly in his chair, eyes darting around the room. I wavered from wanting to embrace the diagnosis to wanting to smother it like a grease fire. When the doctor handed me a Ritalin prescription, I slipped it into my wallet and kept it there like a bullet in the chamber. I could not endorse junk food, but I was supposed to feed him mood-altering drugs whose side effects could potentially damage his heart or turn him into an insomniac? I didn't have the courage to dose him.

Now I am desperate for help. I find a child psychiatrist, a 60-something man who wears cardigan sweaters and wire-rimmed glasses. He is gray and gentle, and he plays basketball with Sym during meetings at his office. Monthly sessions are all I could afford, but they're worth every penny. At his suggestion, I place Sym in the bathroom when his anger flares. The idea is to isolate him in a place where he can't do harm.

"Don't address him when he's angry," the counselor warned me. "He has to learn that it won't solve his problems."

Ignoring my child is the hardest thing I have ever done. Watching him spiral into anger feels like letting a tornado seize him. I pick up my flailing little boy and sit him on the bathroom tiles, pulling the door shut before he can plow into it. I kneel in the hallway with both hands clamped on the knob, sobbing and gasping for air as his feet stomp against the wood veneer. I feel every kick in my throat, against my chest and inside my head. My blood pounds in my ears. I pray the neighbors don't call the complex management or worse — child protective services.

I try to hear the counselor's words in my head over the thumping and wailing.

He has to learn. He has to learn. He has to learn. I repeat it like a mantra and it keeps me steady on the other side of the door.

Later, I enroll him in martial arts when his counselor recommends it. It is another therapy I can scarcely afford, but it is priceless to watch his little body bundled in a clean white dobok, kicking with control. Kicking with a smile.

He is proud of his physical achievements, asking, "How far do you think I can throw this?" when choosing a rock at the park. When he speeds by on his bicycle, he urges me to watch as he pedals up a hill. "Count how many seconds, Mom."

On neighborhood walks, he turns to me suddenly as if set on fire. "Look how fast I can run, Mom," he hollers before shifting into turbo, cheeks flushed as he sprints toward a light post.

"That's incredible," I say.

***

The noise jerks me awake. I open one eye and see my cell pulsating on the nightstand near my bed. I am curled like a warm shrimp inside the eggroll of many blankets. I wriggle an arm out and grab the phone. It's Rawson Elementary.

"This is Sandra from the school office. Symeon is on the playground again and we're going to need you to come…" Before she finishes her plea, I slide out of bed and unfold a pair of socks, shimmy my cold toes inside. I know the drill.

The snowbanks swell outside my window and the fog swirls against the pane. I stand near the front door, thrusting my feet into damp boots, still salt-stained from the morning drop off. The clock says 10:42. It's been just over an hour since I drove the boys to school and raced home for bed. If I'm lucky, five hours of sleep and copious amounts of coffee keep me oiled enough to operate. But not today. My thoughts spiral out of sleep like steam from a boiling pot.

The apartment door clicks shut behind me and when I get in the car it's an icebox. I hit the window button and a blurry sheet of glass slides down. I inhale the frosty glaze of winter air, feel its hypothermic prick. In a daze, I drive to the school and pull up to the lot. Sym is twirling on a swing. He is the only child on the playground, which makes me the only parent. The only divorcee with bedhead, sporting snowflake-patterned pajamas. It is the second time this week I have been called to wrangle him back to the classroom. My feet crunch on the hard-packed snow as I make my way toward him. His hair is windswept and he's not wearing the hat I pulled over his ears this morning. He looks at me, unperturbed.

"Sym," I say, and the word puffs to life in the frigid air. I take a swing beside him and sink into the cold rubber seat. I consider what to say, how to corral him back to his class. It's what I'm supposed to do, but I don't want any part of it. I silently reason with myself. *Couldn't we just go home and hibernate, just the two of us? Couldn't we just climb into bed, pull the blankets up to our eyeballs and forget who we're supposed to be?* The damp ache of winter stretches out across my chest. I want to fall apart with my son.

Two students peer at us from behind a glass pane. They watch us like morning cartoons.

***

The faculty has asked me to medicate him for his ADHD or consider placement in a special class.

"It's a bad idea," Ms. Patrick said in a private meeting. "He's too smart for that class." Those kids aren't on his level, and she thinks they'll drag him down.

Ms. Patrick is Sym's second-grade teacher. For all the headaches he causes, she continues to advocate for my son. This gives me courage, her belief in our collective ability to manage Sym's behavior. When someone dares to empathize with your child, even and especially when he is being unlikable, that person instantly becomes your hero. Such is the case with Ms. Patrick. She keeps the faculty off my back and does her best with the 27 kids in her classroom. But Sym is a beast some days. Even she, with her take-the-bull-by-the-horns-approach, cannot cajole him into submission. So we devise a plan. Based on research that says caffeine can boost concentration for some kids with ADHD, we decide to test the therapeutic potential of a potent cup of joe. Because it's a stimulant drug, caffeine mimics some of the effects of prescription amphetamines used to treat ADHD. Although caffeine alone is less effective, I see it as a hopeful option that is far less scary than a schedule II substance.

I give Sym coffee in the morning and send him to school with Mountain Dew, which the school nurse keeps in her medicine cabinet next to little glass bottles of insulin for the diabetic students. The caffeine takes him down a few notches. He stops whirling in his chair with his shirt pulled over his head, yelling, "I hate this. I HATE this," while the rest of the class pushes pencils on their math tests. He stops shredding papers and storming off to the playground. I want to believe it's not a placebo, but either way it's working.

At a restaurant, KJ gets chocolate milk with a twisty straw while I tell the waitress to pour Sym a cup of regular coffee please — cream and sugar. Her eyebrows arch and I see the questions on her face but I don't explain. I'm tired of explaining. I simply slide the ceramic mug across the table and say, "Thank you."

When the snow melts into soggy chunks and bits, I decide to go for a run. I stomp my way around the park on the cement path that loops around a swing set, a jungle gym and a set of wood-slat benches. With my headphones on, I circle the boys as they flitter like happy birds on the dewy grass. I veer to the right as a woman walks by with a labrador. The dog casts his nose in my direction, a fishing line reeling in my scent. I smile then make a few more laps before returning to the boys. They've mounted the swings again and there is one empty seat. I take it, yank the music from my ears and listen to the swing chains creak as we propel ourselves into the air. High. Higher. Highest. The wind opens up like a hand and lifts us to a new dimension, a weightless bliss where we float together, heads thrown back, tasting the cool of the day. We let our feet dangle, our heads go dizzy. We are dazzled. We eye each other, then pump our legs in a frenzy. High. Higher. Highest, giggling. We are letting go and going nowhere — falling apart in the very best way.

Chapter 8

The Adulterer's Special

I can't find my ex-husband. It's after nine and I'm waiting in the health center parking lot, radio humming, heater firing. The boys are groggy in the backseat, bundled in their bubble coats and knit caps, the tails of their fuzzy scarves trailing. This is our usual spot and I am in my scrubs, ready for my night shift with just a few minutes to spare. I'm getting impatient, tapping my hands on my thighs and sighing as I try to recall our last conversation. "He does know I work tonight, right?" I say to the silent car. *Of course he knows. I told him, I swear I told him. Didn't I?*

All I can think to do is drive to the house we used to share, the house he now occupies alone. I turn the key, check my mirrors, skid across the icy lot. The snow crunches under the tires; the heat sputters through the vents, and my little boys should be in bed.

I pull up and see his Dodge Stratus, apple red and gleaming against the dingy curb snow. I climb the cement steps to the porch where the boys used to crash their toy cars. I hear the ghosts of their summer play, their sandals on the wood planks. When I knock, the porch light beams on and I am standing in a yellow stripe of light, shifting from foot to foot as if I could flick off the cold. I see a shadow in the glass pane, but I can't make it out.

The doorknob turns and I watch the gap widen, revealing a leg, an arm, a face. I don't know this face. It's a woman, twenty-something, tall-ish. Her hair is so red it surprises me. A firetruck thundering from nowhere. I realize my mouth is gaping, nose is dripping. I am a stunned, leaky mom-child.

Sometimes truth crashes down like a dead tree. A splintered, rotted thing, and when you see the enormous carcass, you think, *How did I miss the cracked trunk, all the clues that lay like fallen branches?*

This woman is the culmination of nights my husband worked late in which he was not really working late. She is the secret catalyst for every argument he hurled at me— every cutting glance, the jarring punch of each door slam, the dinners left untouched, congealed, cold and flat. At the core of his restlessness, resistance, growing disdain for our marriage was this redhead in a wrinkled T-shirt. I've known about her, but only in theory. She's the lie I couldn't confirm and was therefore forced to deny. She is good news and bad news — proof I'm not the crazy, overly suspicious woman I've been made to believe I am, proof that J was not merely unhappy with me, but he was happy with her. Happy with this redhead who wears the flannel boxer shorts I bought him. Time slows to a drag while I stand there and swallow hard, understanding for the first time what I have not understood for years: I have been a fool. A blind fool.

A memory floats in. We are in court and the judge has called my husband to the stand. No one expected this, least of all his lawyer. He shoots his attorney a look and she replies with an I-don't-know shrug, then taps her expensive heels on the marble to punctuate the gesture. He makes his way to the hot seat, looking smaller than I've ever seen him look.

"The grass isn't greener on the other side," the judge says as he leans in toward my husband. "Is there someone else?" he asks, stone-faced. I squeeze the tear-soaked tissue in my hand as the room stiffens around me.

"No, sir," my husband says, after a pause that tells us otherwise.

The memory recedes and I stand on the porch, feeling the heat from the house that used to be my house reaching out like fingers to taunt me. The redhead leans against the door so that I can only see a wedge of the dining room, the built-in China cabinet and the polished hardwood floors on which my boys laid on their bellies with fists full of army men, making fighting sounds. All I can think is – *The man I loved did this and everyone knew it but me*. Their faces march into my mind — the roll call of my humiliation. My marriage was a joke of nine years and I have just heard the two-letter punchline: Me.

"He's not home yet," she says. "But I can take the boys so you won't be late for work."

She's hard to read, and at this moment I don't trust my instincts anyway. I can't tell if she's mocking me or trying to be helpful. I know for certain I don't want to be friends with this woman, and there's no way in hell I am leaving my children with her. I turn around to check on them — drowsy in the car under the glow of the lamp post. I swing back to face her, the surprise character in the soap opera of my life.

I ask to use her phone and she steps away then comes back and hands me a cell. I dial my work number and wait while they page the head nurse. Fixing my gaze on the prongs of ice dripping from the railings, I discover her feet. She is wearing the same suede slippers J bought me last Christmas. They came with a matching winter jacket, fur-lined — the color of warm sand. I wonder if she has the jacket too. Does she know we've been dressed alike? Did he get a two-for-one-deal, the adulterer's special?

***

I'm in bed but I can't sleep. Hot tears slide across my face and pool into my ears. It's hard to breathe but I do my best to sob in silence, to mom-cry as I alternately listen for the boys. They exhale in their tiny bedroom next to mine, the long throaty sleep-thrusts of collapsed bundles of energy. They slept through the whole ordeal. J had pulled up to find me on the porch with the mistress and the cell phone. He'd rolled down his window, a dragon roaring breath-smoke in the winter air.

"What the hell are you doing here? I left you three messages. I said I'd be a little late. I told you to meet me outside your work. *Why* are you here?"

His gloved hands went up inside the car to show he'd given up. I'm impossible, an idiot. This infuriated me. I bounded down the cement stairs, slipping on the icy patches and grabbing the metal rail to jolt my body back upright. I stood beside his car.

"How dare you? How daaare you!" I drew out the dare so it became one long, audacious word. I leaned so close, I feared I might get sucked into the quicksand of his anger or the swampy black holes of his eyes. He kept shouting, but I was deaf to the sound. Adrenaline pumped in my ears. I saw his tongue moving wildly in his mouth and it scared me to think how that same snake-flesh roamed my body, caressed my skin. It was like watching a movie, seeing things that were so foreign to me they didn't feel real. And his car: identical to hers. There they were now, side by side in front of the house they shared. The house I'd chosen for us, for my family. How cute is that? I thought about the day he brought the car home and parked it out front without a word. I'd heard him pull up and watched him approach the door, not knowing where he'd been; not knowing that he'd been out test-driving new options.

I'm in bed now, missing work and processing all this. After the shitshow I drove home, hands fixed on the wheel like it could hold me up in the world. But now I am sinking through my mattress into a dark abyss. There is nothing — no past or future for me, at least not the way I imagined it. I have woken up in a world I don't recognize and now I must navigate in unfamiliar terrain.

***

Betrayal is a physical assault. The pain rips into me with unrelenting force. It swims in my veins and swells beneath my skin like a bruise that has broken every capillary. It colors me deep purple. I am a full-body bruise.

I wonder everything about her — J's mistress. What does she call him: babe, baby, honey, sweetie, boo? I never used pet names. I was an introverted wife. The girl who changed clothes in the closet, who gave hugs sparingly, who spent every effort on housekeeping, mothering, stretching the dollars we earned. I had leaped from girlhood to motherhood and was working to assimilate my womanhood.

I find her on social media and learn she's a sports fan like him. A *meat and potatoes kind of girl* — her words, not mine. I don't like football, basketball, baseball, crowded arenas or hot dogs from sweaty street vendors. I like my son in his martial arts uniform, and if this is a sport, it's the only one I have ever grown to love. When I think about J's mistress, I wonder if my lack of interest in sports has anything to do with the death of our marriage. If I'd made an effort to cheer for his team, to understand the plays, to roar, "Come on, defense," what might have been different for us?

I wonder if she bakes, reads, cleans, takes bubble baths before bed like I do. I wonder if she wears makeup, sundresses, pajamas with pretty lace hems. Does she make the bed or leave the blankets in a heap on the mattress? Does she grumble when she finds the coils of his beard hairs sprinkled all over the sink? Is she a cuddler, a hold-me-at-night kind of woman? These thoughts make me cringe, but I can't stop imagining their union, their attraction, their evenings at home together. I need to know why I was so bad and she was so good, if that's what drove this affair. In my broken mind, I think maybe if I can learn about her, I can learn about me, about all the things I couldn't understand when I was married to an unhappy man. I am crazy for answers. She's a textbook I need to read: *Men Are from Mars, and So Are Their Lovers*.

***

Just before I met and married J, a friend invited me out on Halloween. I wore tight jeans and a Lycra top, red lipstick and loads of hair gel. Not an actual costume, but a typical date-me ensemble. The friend pulled up in her black Maxima, beeped in my driveway. I got in the car, thrift-store boots crunching on empty fast-food takeout bags. With '90s jams shaking the windows and the eye of her Newport cigarette blazing in the dark, we sped off. She drove us to the south side of Milwaukee and we pulled up in front of a house, beeped the horn and waited, wailing along with Janet Jackson.

"*Cute* bracelets," I said as she tapped out a beat on the steering wheel. Without a word, she poked her half-smoked menthol into her mouth and squinted behind a curl of smoke. I watched her pull off three of the six beaded bangles on her wrist and hand them to me.

Two songs later, a thin blonde emerged from the brick two-story, dressed like a prisoner in a striped jail suit.

"Ha!" I said aloud then followed it up with an actual laugh as the girl squeezed in the backseat. "Great costume." She smiled and told me her name was Jessica and that she was sorry it took her so long.

"I have twin boys," she explained, rolling her eyes.

Inside, the bar was an ashtray, stale and thick with smoke. The tables were wobbly and round with ripped leather stools all around. Wide-eyed, middle-aged men looked up from their beers, their eyes fondling our curves. I followed my friends to a table where a mustached man in a cowboy hat brought us drinks. No one questioned our ages. Seedy bars were hot spots for underagers like us. But secretly, I preferred house parties with teens who stuffed family photos in drawers and let their dogs lick remnants of Cheetos off the carpet.

We danced a little and I watched the red lights bloom like poppies all over the dance floor. Breathless and woozy, we returned to a table where random men with stubble and deep voices came over to flash their teeth and try out their lines. I relied on my jukebox savvy — turning away from the men who made my skin bristle to follow the beats, belt out choruses and take off suddenly with a friend's hand in mine, carried by a song.

At some point, my friends motioned me outside where Cowboy Hat led us into the lobby of an apartment complex next door. The door shut behind him and we stood there in the tiny room, the staircase behind us. I leaned up against a brick wall and listened to the music thud from the bar. The man reached into his pocket and pulled out a tiny glass bottle. Cocaine. He held it up in the low light and I turned my head as my friends huddled closer to take their hits. I must have looked disgusted because no one prodded me to indulge. Drinks were enough for me. I watched Jessica's feet, her legs, the prisoner stripes as she leaned in to snort a line. I saw my hand go up to stop her, to pull her away from the poison but my fingers froze at my side. I thought about her twin boys at home, waiting up for Mommy. I thought about what it means to want a mother who wants her own life. Her very own life.

I never saw those friends again, but I think about them often, and the things I left behind. I traded up, I thought — dank bars and bad company for a guy who never drank or partied but would drive me clear to Chicago for good pizza. And then we'd drive some more with the windows down and no destination, the sky like a velvet curtain. Five dollars in the console and dreams that couldn't fail. You couldn't tell me I wasn't lucky.

"I can see us married," he'd said after just a month. And when I closed my eyes, I saw it too. Three months later, we were. Now we're divorced and I'm lying here like roadkill, only I'm not dead.

***

"Oh what a tangled web we weave
when first we practice to deceive."
~ Walter Scott

I don't know how she heard the news, whether it came by a phone call or a visit from a stone-faced stranger, but someone told my mother this: Your husband is molesting your children. Perhaps she rolled it over in her head, like a chef with a hunk of dough, pounding out the lumps. At some point, she decided to make it a lie.

Later, we sat in a room. Our eyes were oceans apart, adrift on separate islands. A woman put a doll on my lap, a strange and faceless doll that was really a prop.

"Show us," she prodded. "Show us where he touched you."

I did what she asked, although I was heavy with shame and my hands were concrete in my lap.

"Did he insert..." she started to say, then paused to observe me before beginning again. "Do you know the meaning of insert?" I did. And for a moment, I was proud. I wanted to tell her all the words I knew and that I was a champion speller. I wanted to talk about the books I read and the characters in my head. I wanted to tell her how I lived inside those books, like a caterpillar. They were my cocoon. But we didn't talk about that. We talked instead about ugly things, things that made me shift in my chair, stare at the rug and wish it would all go away. It didn't matter what I said because after counseling sessions and visits from curious people who clutched their files and clipboards, my mother found her own cocoon. She spun new stories and invented a set of characters we could become. When it was time to return home, I slipped into my old bed, bleary-eyed and confused. Alone in the dark, I wondered if he would come again. I never stopped wondering.

When he filled my bicycle tires with air or greased its rusty chain, she said, "Look what your dad did!" And though he was not my father and my real dad was long gone, I pretended. I played the character she created, the girl she could love. When he eyed me from the sofa, opened his bathrobe and flashed his anatomy, I sat beside my mother who watched her favorite show. I let those moments curl away like black smoke in my memory as I listened to the Tracy Ullman theme song. And the years passed as my mother reminded us all: *This is a happy home.*

***

After discovering J's mistress, I think about my mother, about the cobwebs she spun in her memory, her net of self-protection, her shelter from the truth. I think about the lies I chose because reality was too much to bear. *My husband is a sports fan and he likes to watch games at the sports bars after work,* I'd convinced my inner doubts. *We sleep in separate beds because we work opposite shifts. It's easier this way. Besides, who has time for romance?* When a friend said he spotted him at the mall with another woman, I told him it must have been someone else, a man who looks like my husband. No, he's not a great mate, but he's a pretty good dad. A diaper-changing, cartoon-watching dad. His moods? They are murky but manageable. Nobody's perfect, and forgiveness is good for the soul. We are a happy family, and this is a happy home.

Chapter 9

A Move in The Right Direction

I am having one of those days in which there is too much and too little. Too much stress, too little sleep. Too many thoughts of J and the redhead unraveling in my brain like a spool of pulled thread. One thought stretches into another. I imagine them together on the nights when he worked late and I waited up with a warm dinner plate. Stupid, stupid me. I hate that it hurts. I want to be stronger than I am, smarter than I was. I have the feeling that my skin is a barbed wire fence and I want to crawl out of myself entirely.

A child wails. It's my child, my 8-year-old son KJ. He is experiencing a crisis worthy of high-pitched whining, tears and a fantastic display of anger. I follow the sound to the bedroom where 6-year-old Sym watches from the top bunk. It's not his bed, but he's no fool. It's a small room and while toys can be flung, the safest place to hide from a rabid sibling is always the top bunk bed — depending, of course, on your mother's willingness to respond to your screams. As a middle child, I know this from experience. Sym's pleading eyes tell me he is the culprit and the crime he's committed is worse than any territorial dispute that could arise. He's willing to roll the dice.

"What's going on?" I say, taking the mom stance — hands on hips, chin jutting into the room. KJ can't speak. His little face glistens like a new penny, tears tumbling down. He has a Darth Vader helmet at his feet, a Christmas gift from last year. He bends over, picks it up. It's black and shiny, an electronic headpiece with flat eye screens and a grate for a mouth.

"He wouldn't let me play with it," Sym pipes in from behind us, then slinks back into his corner.

This supplies KJ with a jolt of outrage. "He pooped in my mask," he hollers, thrusting the helmet in my face.

I take the soiled toy, inspect it. "Where?"

"Inside," KJ says, "and I put it on my face." More tears come with the word "face" as if it's all too much to bear. His cheeks crumple and his eyes become sad little half-moons.

He shoots Sym a look, to which Sym replies once more, "You wouldn't let me play with it!"

***

My kids are the kind of terrible that really isn't terrible. But it's damn sure memorable.

Some Memories

It was quiet. That should have been my first clue that something was amiss. I am 3 chapters in and it's a page-turner. We spent the morning grocery shopping, which in itself is not a high-impact workout but if you wrangle two boys with four lanky arms vying for the marshmallows and Frosted Flakes, you end up winded. We followed the trip up with a visit to the library and now I'm in front of the window in my comfy chair with a cup of reheated coffee and this paperback. All is well until I see the neighbor from across the street making her way toward my house. Her neck is craned upward as if she's inspecting the clouds for rain. It's an odd posture, and when she drops her head back down to eye level, I see disappointment in her gaunt face. I'd like to pretend we're not home, but she sees me leaning toward the window as she thumps up the steps and onto our porch. There are no hellos.

"Are your boys allowed to play on the roof?" She stammers. She's a hard woman with nicotine-stained fingertips and eyes like polished blades.

"Excuse me?"

"Your boys are on the roof right now. I saw them from across the street." She points to the spot where she witnessed the crime — her porch, where a plastic chair sits next to a matching table and loaded ashtray. "The older one told me it was okay because *YOU* said they could play up there." I release the door and it bangs shut as I race upstairs. I take the steps three at a time and find KJ's window wide open. The sheer curtain flutters against the sill and the outside spills in. Everything is sun kissed and smells like sticks and grass and leaves. It's the kind of day I could inhale deeply. I shove my head out and hear KJ before I see him.

"No, Symeon, Spiderman does this..." he says. I spot him on the flat part of the roof, wearing his Spiderman pajamas and a blanket he's knotted at the neck like a cape. His bony fingers demonstrate the web-shooter method: forefingers, thumbs and pinkies firing. Sym stands beside him, cape-blanket sagging around his neck. His plump bottom lip pokes out as he fumbles with his fingers. He is shirtless and wearing a pair of cartoon boxer shorts. It's pushing 60 degrees and the wind shows up in his hair, rippling every curl. It's a long way down. I can see the ocean floor of everything, the sidewalk beside the house and the whole block if I stretch out my neck:

the messy shrubs like tangled seaweed, the shingled roofs like dirty fish scales. There is the school and the stop sign on the corner where kids lump together until the traffic passes. I wonder how they'd look from here, like spinning tops or maybe confetti. There is the neighbor who thinks I'm a terrible mother. She's back in her plastic chair with a cigarette in her hand. Smoke billows up, spreads out and glides into the blue afternoon.

I look down again at my wayward superheroes. They are far from the edge of the roof so there's no chance they'll plummet to the ground. I allow them another few seconds to savor the penthouse views, and then I'll give them hell.

Another memory

How does KJ know the bro code? He is a scrawny grade-schooler who ties his shoes with loops like Dumbo's ears. And while he protects his brother, he is quick to pimp him out too.

"Ask Mom for ice cream," he whispers. Or "Put these cookies down your shirt." Or "Tell her you did it — it was an accident!"

One Monday, post-weekend-wrestling-match-gone-wrong, KJ's teacher inquires about the purple ring around his eye. The right answer would have been: This is where the wall interfered when my brother rocketed me off his back. But that was not the option he chose. Instead, he replied without hesitation, "My mom punched me in the face."

After school, the doorbell rings. I glance through the peephole and see a woman with hair like whipped potatoes wearing a wool blazer and clutching a briefcase. I wonder what she's selling. I almost don't answer but I'm curious.

She is Beverly with a business card or a badge. I'm not sure which because she is nudging her way inside and telling me she's with CPS, child protective services. The boys are blabbering on kitchen chairs, bent over a table snaked with cars.

"Nooo! *This* is the fastest car, Sym," KJ says, replacing a blue car with a black car in their lineup.

Beverly tells me she needs to chat with KJ alone and asks where they can talk. I point her to the living room and watch them leave the kitchen. I am willing my ears to hear, pinching my eyes shut and listening with force. I've crept as close to the living room as I can get and I lean against the wall, angling my head toward their voices like a radar gun.

"Vroooom," Sym hollers from the table, happy to lead the crew in KJ's absence.

As I watch Sym's chubby feet slap the chair legs, it occurs to me that KJ may be wearing holey socks. I can't explain the sock situation in this house. It's a mystery even to me. Socks get washed, put on feet and the shoes go on. But they often return with stinky toes punched out, like worms after a storm. I'm biting my hand now, wondering if KJ's toes are on display as Beverly takes notes with her heavy brass pen. And I don't know yet what he's told his teacher, but I assume the black eye is the reason for this visit. Now if my son can just tell her how it happened...

It's like she's buying the house. When they return from their chat, Beverly stomps into every room, her chunky black pumps click on the floor as she opens the pantry, examines the food then moves on. She writes it all down, flushes the toilets. They gurgle and groan. She smiles.

"Okay," she finally says, scribbling a few more notes before lowering her clipboard and looking me in the eye. She tells me what happened at school, how the teacher had to report it because she's required to; it's protocol.

"I see the artwork on the refrigerator," she says, pointing to the messy watercolor handprint. I almost blurt out I didn't do it, that my art is much better than that, but she continues. "We look for this kind of stuff. The race car bed, the pantry full of snacks, the toys — all signs of a good home. I'll have to come back again but don't be concerned. It's all routine."

I walk her to the door and just as it shuts I hear KJ roar from the kitchen, "Mom, Sym said he wants dinner now-wwww."

I watch Beverly duck into her little white car. This would be the best time to punch KJ in the face.

***

It will be just us now, the boys and me. No dad in proximity. The out-of-state moving service charges per square foot. It's a number so high I have to lean in and cock my head. "Excuse me?" I say, because I can't believe my ears. But it's slightly cheaper than starting over with all new furniture. And besides, I am in no mood to sell what I've got, to host a garage sale and haggle with strangers who clip coupons for sport and already have too many toasters and bed frames. So I decide to sell just a few items that take up space. A woman and her husband respond to my Craigslist posting and come over to test out my treadmill. They ask why I'm getting rid of the thing when I've told them I use it almost daily. "I'm moving to Florida," I say, as if it's a dream come true, as if I've got a beach house waiting, a couple of friends already slathering tanning oil on their shoulders, cheering, "She'll be here by this time next week," and sipping margaritas in the sun.

"That's exciting!" the woman exclaims. She's in her forties, newly diagnosed with MS. It's the reason they are treadmill shopping, her husband told me on the phone.

"Yes," I say, "it is."

This woman has an incurable disease, so I don't heap my half-pint misery on her by telling her the whole story — the part about the home I rented sight unseen in a city I've only visited on the internet. Braver people might find that riveting, but for me, it's just plain terrifying. I don't say my real goal is to put 1,200 miles between my ex-husband and me. To give myself that much space to think and breathe and move untethered.

It's been four years since our divorce, and I can't adjust to single motherhood with him in close range. Blame it on too many *Leave It to Beaver* episodes, but I couldn't see us being whole without him. I could bake rigatoni with cheese until it bubbled and browned, but I couldn't get the boys to stop flinging dinner off their forks, launching noodles at one another. J could, with a look, with sturdy shoulders that didn't slump like mine. Every evening I tried to conjure his dad magic, but I simply did not have it. And if by chance he appeared at bedtime, I was reminded of this. He could swoop in and make a sporting event of our evening fiasco. If the boys were whining about undressing, he'd have them racing to peel off their socks and shimmy out of school clothes in record time. And just like that, all my frustrations vanished. I appreciated his help, but it didn't come free.

Within a few years of our divorce, J had lost his job, the house, his mistress. One night his car spun out on black ice then flipped into a ditch on the side of the highway. He kicked his way out through the windshield and later realized his insurance had lapsed. He'd lost his car too. These events happened like some eerie karmic explosion, sending him lumbering back in my life as if struck by an epiphany. Since I aspired to repair our family, we agreed to counseling. We spent hopeful nights making plans. I thought the glue of more time might hold us together for good. But time is no glue, and after 13 years I finally realized I'd given him too much.

I had imagined living in the Sunshine State, leaving all my winter storms behind, the ice of everything. I called my mother often, and despite the ways she failed me, I longed to be near her. You only get one mother, imperfections and all.

"I'm wearing flip-flops today," she teased after she'd moved to Florida. "I bet you're wearing boots."

When she sent me photos of a rental house in her neighborhood, I mentally began to pack. If I stayed in Wisconsin, I was sure J would be back at my door in a week, a month or a year, lamenting his mistakes. He'd come with a new blueprint for our family. There were so many blueprints. Even as he rolled them out, I'd see the bitter end. But I couldn't trust my memory to recall how the past had been, to remind me that his charm was a mirage.

"I feel I'm losing myself," I tell a friend over coffee one afternoon. I imagine a flower dropping its petals — less of me every day. The newness of a life without J scares me, and my desire to give our boys the nuclear family dynamic keeps thrusting me back to him. But now, in a moment of clarity, I break the news. "I'm moving to Florida."

Florida

We are bickering over boxes in our sunny living room. "Who took the hammer?" I bellow, taking a step forward and landing on the rusty claw buried beneath clumps of packing paper.

"I need the hammer," KJ declares, waving his skinny brown arm in the air.

"You absolutely do *not* need the hammer," I say.

"But I want to hang this." He unrolls a glossy *Lord of the Rings* poster and holds it up, smiling. I notice the neat stack of his collectibles and clothing, which he has already found and unpacked. This child is methodical, my door-knob-polishing, storage-bin-stacking son. On the opposite end of the gene pool, young slovenly Sym makes a splash. They are eleven and nine, and their new school is right across the street.

Sym has emptied the contents of a large box on the carpet and climbed inside. Fashioning weapons out of wads of packing tape, he tosses the sticky bombs in the air and mimics the sounds of a blast, "Peowww, peowww."

In a few days, he'll be settled in with accidental science projects under his bed: food-crusted plates and juice-stained cups, which eventually will become public housing for various insects. We had talked about Florida bugs, about palmetto bugs so big they could bitch slap a dog.

"Forget about Goldilocks," I told him. "If you don't clean your room in Florida, a giant cockroach will steal your bed."

He'll believe it when he sees it, he says.

When the quiet of evening descends, I saunter into their shared room while they sleep. The curtains are parted and the backyard stretches out to the road. There is so much open space and the trees are husky and graceful, with moss tangled up like wild hair. I can see the whole sky, rolled out like a clean silk sheet and unencumbered by city lights, apartment complexes or corporate buildings. This is not Milwaukee. Out here there is nothing but me, my sons, the sky. The door is cracked just enough to allow a vein of light in from the hall. It settles on their faces, their silky eyelashes and dreamy open mouths. I listen to the sounds of their sleep as the ceiling fan spins overhead. My mind spins too.

When I was an 18-year-old girl, life was cold, so I picked up a husband and put him on like an overcoat. But now I am a 32-year-old woman and it's time to strip down, set myself free. I have to find out who I can be without J — without even the possibility of him.

***

I can't write. I mean, it's physically possible but I am creatively defunct. This is a problem because if I don't write, we don't eat. Plus, there's no child support. It's what I agreed to so J would allow me to take the boys out of state. He was in arrears already and more than happy to oblige under these terms. I thought I had a handle on freelancing. Prior to moving, I'd worked myself up to full-time writing. I started with some college courses online and I learned the basics: How to write a query letter, hook a reader with a compelling lede, show versus tell. Then I got my first clip when a small magazine published a story I'd written about hospital work. The brown envelope came in the mail with a thank-you letter and a copy of the story in shiny ink.

"Look boys," I said. "Here's my name!" I marveled at the sight of it — my name on a page in a magazine. A writer. Soon after, I landed a freelance gig for a large media company. For two years, I wrote online content whenever I peeled off my scrubs. I left the healthcare facility and rushed home to tap at my keyboard. In the early mornings or late into the night, I researched and wrote health articles about medications, symptoms, fad diets. I told people how to cure athlete's foot, about the stages of Alzheimer's disease, and how to whip up a meal plan for the cabbage soup diet. I knew it wasn't serious journalism, but I was working under real editors, working toward something. I was learning how to turn a phrase. It was thrilling and nerve-racking at once. It was tilling my creative soil, plucking word-seeds from my brain and planting ideas on the page. I wondered if I could grow something beautiful one day. Something memorable — a book.

I'd always loved wordplay and poetry and library day at school when I was a kid. On Tuesdays, I could check out Nancy Drew mysteries or Beverly Cleary books. While my siblings rode bikes in summer or watched cartoons in the living room, I hovered over my paperbacks like a honey bee sucking nectar. Inspired by my favorite authors, I fashioned my own books from cardboard and wrapping paper and presented them to my grandmother, who fawned over all my creations. When I was 11 years old, my school essay garnered an award. I was selected to attend a conference at the Milwaukee Art Museum where successful authors spoke about their careers to a crowd of budding writers. I imagined myself on the stage wearing something writerly: a tailored pantsuit, a pair of expensive heels. I'd be addressing the crowds one day. I'd be an author.

I look around now at our little Florida home and there is nothing left to unpack. There are no curtains to hang, beds to make, towels to stack on fresh shelves. There is no more frenzied pace to keep me from the business of living my new life. Every bit of work is done now, yet there is so much to do. I have everything to do.

The clock blinks and the silence in my mind bumps around with fear. If I can't awaken my brain, I will have to find alternate work. I imagine myself in a food-stained apron, pouring coffee into cheap porcelain mugs. *Will work for tips.*

***

Routine — I decide that's what I need. All the pros have some sort of ritual in which they partake, a means to rouse the muse. After the boys leave for school, I sip coffee in my pink flowery mug near the window. I try to make it meaningful, to decode the banter of the neighborhood birds as if it held some esoteric insights. My notebook sits idly beside me with yesterday's assignments unexplored. A blank doc is open on my computer, but it mocks me, mirroring the space in my head. No words or ideas come to me, and I fear they are gone forever. *Where are my words?*

Last night I dreamed I was a singer approaching the stage in a cascading gown. With coiffed hair and makeup shimmering beneath the lights, I scanned the arena, noting the endless clusters of bodies like wildflowers in a field. Silence rippled through the room. Hundreds of eyes were pinned to me. Stepping toward the microphone, I wrapped my hand around it and opened my mouth to the crowd. But there was nothing. No sound. I was hollow.

**

It's been three weeks since we left Wisconsin, and J is out of touch.

"He's probably working a lot," I tell the boys. "I'm sure he misses you like crazy."

KJ nods in agreement but Sym does not buy it. He has an ultra-sensitive bullshit meter, and this lie trips his alarm. Ripping his pillow from behind him, he presses it against his face to mask his tears.

"Call him," he growls.

"I've called him already and we'll just have to wait now," I say.

"Something is wrong. Something bad happened to him, I just know it." His hand inches out from under his blanket and finds mine. "Pray for my dad," he says.

I've run out of prayers. Out of patience, out of words.

Dear God, make the phone ring.

**

Sym is shirtless in the yard, bug-bitten and bronzed, whacking a stick at a tree.

It's getting late and I have asked him to come in three times. Finally, he heeds my fourth call, thrashing the tree once more before laboring inside.

"I think you need a shower," I say. "Please put your clothes in the washer."

He sneers and tramps into the garage, where the washer and dryer sit side by side on a concrete slab. I go back to chopping peppers — red, yellow and green, a festive pile of veggies the boys will drown in ranch dressing. I hear a crash, a bang, a roar. I drop my knife and rush in to find my son, red-faced and hurling a spare tire at the garage wall. His hair is sweaty and juts up like an animal in defense mode.

"Sym," I yell.

He reloads, grabbing items from an open box. He lobs a flashlight and it cracks apart, explodes in jagged bits. I watch the contents of a toolbox skid across the room: a screwdriver, a hammer, a plastic pack of nails. One, two, three picture frames crack on the concrete, the high-pitched ting of breaking glass sounds like wind chimes in a storm. I watch my child whirl, the Tasmanian Devil.

"Sym," I plead. "Sym…" The more I try to engage him, the angrier he gets. I can't call his dad, but I know a man he will talk to.

Anthony is a blue-jeans-wearing, late-twenties youth pastor, father and husband. Tall, with herculean hands and a smile that glides up to his ears. We met him at the little church down the street and quickly learned we were neighbors. I'm watching Nickelodeon with KJ when he comes over to chat with Sym in the living room. I hear their muffled voices over the show I'm pretending to watch, but I can't make out the words. I decide to just be grateful Sym is talking again.

When they finish their discussion, an hour has passed and Anthony pokes his head in the doorway and says, "Just wanted to say goodnight."

I get up, walk him to the door and fight the urge to ask him for a play-by-play since Sym is eyeing me from the couch. He looks like my kid again. No more sweaty tufts of hair. No more frenetic motion. His face is serene and he reaches for Anthony's hand. They shake.

"See you at youth group," Anthony says. "And don't forget — ice cream afterward, you and me." He smiles and I thank him as he exits, throwing me a look I read as, *It's going to be fine.*

At midnight I'd rather be sleeping, but when I close my eyes I see Sym's fiery cheeks, him hurling the tire in the garage. I get up and amble into the other room where I flick on the light near my desk. I open a document and begin pecking out my pain and frustration. I write a letter to J, to God, to myself and to no one at all. I type and I type and I type. My fingers against the keys, striking, striking, striking. Twenty-six letters making an ocean of words. I am a swimmer, diving into word waves, fingers plunging into the deep. I pour it all onto the page, all the internal clutter, and it feels like the adult version of slinging tires.

When the page is full, I see all the messy bits — my broken dreams for a love that was doomed to fail, my impossible faith in the family we could not be, the prayers that couldn't save us. I watch my hands tremble over the keyboard. At last, my fingers are nimble. My mind is clear.

***

Carlo is an eccentric Chihuahua with an inflated sense of self. While he is afraid of the reflection in his stainless-steel water bowl, he makes zealous attempts to take down the larger breeds: gangly Dobermans, German shepherds and obese mastiffs. We end up with him a month after moving to Florida. I realize the boys could use a new friend to help smooth the transition. He is five pounds and in need of a new home when a college girl and her boyfriend drive him over on a Sunday night. I am sitting outside, watching the bugs thump their wings on the gleaming orb of the patio light. The street is a black stripe out front, which the occasional car illuminates as it whizzes past at 60 or higher. This excites the boys, who are eagerly watching from inside, faces pressed on the window like postage stamps. I'll handle it, I tell them. The dog deal is a transaction after all, and anxious kids will both drive up the price and upset the dog. I have a crisp $50 in my pocket. And after that, there will be a trip to the pet store and vet bills, so this isn't going to be cheap.

"A dog is a real commitment, kids. You get it?" They nod, eyes bright as holiday bulbs.

I spend the most time with Carlo, our cantankerous little beast. He doesn't let me hold him. Instead, he crouches in a corner and watches me from across the room, flashing a pair of clean incisors whenever I get too close. I ignore him and instruct the boys to do the same. I understand his distrust, his need to guard his heart.

"He'll come around," I say, hoping I am right.

As I move through the house, I feel his eyes like little black beams boring into me while I pour my coffee, wash the morning dishes or sit at my desk and wait for the computer to blaze to life. Inch by inch, he creeps closer until he successfully pins himself to me, a scraggy dog-ribbon. An unexpected prize.

Having Carlo makes me realize how much we need him. At 3:05, I click on his leash and we amble up the street, his little tail flapping like a flag in the sunshine. He leads me through the afternoon mayhem, the backpacked kids zigzagging on bicycles and mothers pushing strollers on the sidewalk. When we spot Sym, Carlo shoots toward him, a dog-bullet in the crowd.

At night, he burrows between me and the mattress. I never invite him, but one restless evening he hops up, and though he is small, he seems to fill an awful chasm. He keeps me from flailing as the patter of his tiny heartbeat plays like a lullaby. In the morning, he paws me awake so we can start the day together. How odd that my sons' dog, whose sole purpose in our home is to bolster *their* spirits, ends up bolstering mine. Carlo helps me navigate the lonely terrain of single motherhood, but he becomes attached to my mother's dog. When I take him over for a visit, he eases his way into her household. One morning as I'm repainting the front door of our home, he slips past me and bolts across the street and through the neighbor's yard. He finds his rust-haired partner in crime: Rudy, a long-haired Chihuahua with an overbite. This is my mother's dog, and together the two raise hell yapping at manic squirrels. In her house, they perch on the back of the sofa near the window, the ivory tower where they watch for mail carriers and other intrusive passersby.

Carlo begins spending nights with Rudy, and these evenings stretch on indefinitely. Carlo has made his choice.

Chapter 10

My Soul is a Paper Ship

It's getting harder to pray. Or maybe I'm getting harder, calcified. Still, I force myself into rituals, hoping to revive the faith I've nursed for more than a decade. The pastor asked for volunteers to help clean the church offices on Saturdays. I silently committed to the task. I need to get more involved, I tell myself. But it takes me a few weeks to actually show up. I stand in the lobby feeling awkward because I'm sporting a paint-stained tank top and sloppy hair in church. It feels sacrilegious and I have the urge to explain my outfit to the Jesus painting in the foyer. The lights are off but the sun is bright and shadows stretch out on the tiles like sleeping dogs in the hall. It looks like no one is here, except I see soapy spots of water on the floor and I hear music coming from the sanctuary. I follow the sound and find Anthony wearing shorts and a T-shirt, swishing a broom to the beat of the stereo.

"Hey," he says, looking up as I hop around wet spots.

"Sorry to screw up your floor," I say.

"No problem." He smiles. "You wanna start in the kitchen?" he asks, pointing to the tiny room behind the sanctuary where a coffee pot, refrigerator and pantry huddle in a closet-sized space.

"Sure," I say as I tiptoe across the room. He hollers that it needs to be swept and wiped down. All the supplies are on the counter.

A few hours later, we're sticky and achy. I hear the double doors bang shut and see Anthony's wife approach with their toddler. She pushes a vacuum cleaner to one side of the room and kicks the cord beside it.

"The nursery is finished," she announces.

We chat while arranging chairs for the Sunday service. I don't mention it, but I'm surprised that no one else has shown up to help, not even the pastor who gave a nice speech about acts of service when he lobbied for help with the spring cleaning. I want to be a selfless giver, but I go home feeling angry and used. I have all these emotions that keep popping up, and trying to fight them back is like a game of Wack-A-Mole. I ask God for help, but my feelings grow bigger. My body becomes unruly and I stop attending church because my mouth won't sing the hymns and my hands won't fold to pray. Three months pass and I don't leave the house except to buy groceries or take walks at night with the boys. *I work from home*, I tell myself. *I'm working*. But when the boys leave for school, I curl up on the sofa or head back to bed and pull a blanket over my face. I get up again at noon and sit in my chair near the window. I think about the way I used to pray, how prayer became a song that never left my lips. I could hum from my heart straight to heaven, and it brought me strength or peace. But there's no music now, and I don't trust the lyrics.

One Sunday, the doorbell rings. It takes me a moment to squint through the light. The sun is so bright it's blinding.

When my eyes adjust, I see Anthony and his wife on the stoop. They see me too and smile. I don't want to be seen. I'm in my pajamas as usual, and it's late afternoon. I hesitate, then open the door limply. I am a dishrag. I pull on a wobbly smile and they sit on the loveseat with faces that say, *We're concerned.* I pretend not to see their parental expressions. I tell them how busy I am with work, how I keep odd hours because I like to write at night, which is partially true. I write late because it takes half the day to get motivated. Because my feelings weigh me down and it's hard to move.

"Do you think you'll come back to church?" they ask in unison. It's a tag-team effort.

I want to say yes because I want to be like them: confident, beaming God-orbs. But I'm beginning to wonder if I can trust the God I thought I knew, or the church, or the woman I was on the pew — the woman who prayed and stayed in a broken marriage because she thought it was God's plan, the woman who listened to all the voices in the room and forgot how to hear her own. Forgot she even had a voice.

"Thanks for the invitation," I say. "But I need to spend Sundays alone."

***

When I meet a man from Chandigarh, India, my worldview changes. Mani is a friend of a friend, whom I commissioned for website design work. We email at first, about work and the specifics of my project. And then one Friday evening he calls to ask a question. I am divvying up Chinese takeout — cartons of fried rice and paper-wrapped egg rolls. Without thinking, I ask a random question. "What do you eat in Chandigarh?"

"Naan," Mani says. "With lentils and vegetables." Masala, he tells me, is a blend of spices that flavors the food, mostly cumin, cinnamon, cardamom, black pepper and cloves. He is friendly and chatty, and as curious about America as I am about India. As he describes golden daals, rich gravies and curried rice dishes, I forget about my own hot plate. I kick back and listen as Chandigarh materializes in my mind: rickshaws zigzagging in the streets, food vendors manning steaming pots on roadside stands. We continue to talk, about books, television shows and the quirks and contrasts in our cultures. Soon we become each other's tour guides, connecting via email, Skype and text messages. Mani is smart and silly. When his face appears on my screen, his beard is black and thick as fur, a teddy bear of a man who smiles, recites poems and gushes over philosophy and art. He teaches me Punjabi words and songs and sends me videos of his life: birthday celebrations with friends and cooking mishaps in his kitchen. His laughter shakes something loose in me, the walls of a woman in hiding. I feel myself being transported right out of my life, across oceans where women wear ornate saris and musicians strum the twangy sitar. I love the music so much, Mani sends me dozens of YouTube videos every day.

"This is enchanting, like hearing music again for the first time," I say as we watch together on separate continents. There are hymns and wrenching ballads. I can't understand the lyrics, but somehow they speak to me. At night, I replay the songs in my dark room, the mysterious words and undulations, rising, falling, vibrating like a rung bell.

I teach Mani Scrabble, and we play for hours over the computer. He beats me most games and we laugh, me the writer, him the foreigner, kicking my ass with the English language.

We cry together too. Mani is heartbroken over the death of his fiancée, Ruby, who'd entered the hospital with a virus two years prior. He has his grief and I have my disappointment and crumbling faith, emotions that drive us to solitude. But solitude together. We are two souls in hibernation, spanning the distance between us, and it is exactly what we need.

A follower of Sikh, Mani rises early to go to the temple and pray. I can always tell when he's been there. His face lightens; he appears childlike as if he's shed a decade. He talks about the presence of God, of his religion and its tenets. So spiritual, he is, and devout.

"So what do you think... am I going to hell?" he asks one day, eyebrows mocking.

Mani can recite the Bible, and he knows the precepts of Christianity: One God, one truth. There is one way to heaven — I believed that. Suddenly, I don't anymore. When I see Mani's face, I can't fathom a fiery hell, and the more I examine my beliefs, the stranger they look to me, like foreign objects.

At night, I pull books off my shelf, surf the internet, stumble about for answers. I am drunk with confusion and staggering between two worlds, neither of which feels like home. Omnipotent, omnipresent, somehow it doesn't add up. If God sees everything, how can he simply watch? What kind of father is he? Children starving. Terrorists bombing. Gunmen invading school classrooms. And God watching? If God is perfect, all powerful, the essence of love, how can he be apathetic, too? These thoughts make loops in my brain, along with the scriptures that used to comfort me: *God will never leave us nor forsake us. God is our refuge and strength, an ever-present help in times of trouble.* I recite these lines as if they are spells, as if I can bewitch myself back to belief. A part of me is afraid to let my faith go, so I hold on like the little girl who gripped the blankets at night and prayed against the footsteps in the bedroom, against the naked man looming near the bed. But God didn't save. Why didn't he? An old wound reopens, the salt of abandonment stinging me anew. Am I the girl of my youth, finding the voice to scream? Burned by fathers, the clergy, a husband,

I have been set on fire. In a moment of weakness (or is it clarity?) I have the courage to say I don't know who God really is. My quest to learn everything has shown me I know nothing. I am done with blind faith, with platitudes like *God works in mysterious ways*. I want a god who isn't mysterious, an undeniable god. I lie in bed and feel the ash beneath me, the remnants of a faith-life. I drift into sleep hoping that when I awaken, I will somehow awaken.

***

Eighty-eight books. I stack them in sturdy piles in my bedroom, tall as baby trees, and I think with a tinge of sadness: *so long, old self.* Each title, a plea for self-improvement. I was desperate to become a bolder believer, a powerful praying momma, the woman who fixed my family. I have always maintained the idea that if you want to know about a person, all you have to do is peek at her bookshelves. But these spiritual books no longer feel like mine, so I cram them into boxes with itchy sweaters and old heels for donation. It's irrational, I know, but somehow I feel these books have betrayed me by not delivering the results I'd imagined. Now they are simply reminders of all my failed attempts. Clothes and shoes are things I imagined I'd outgrow. But my religion? I never thought one day I would toss it in a box.

In a sermon in the early years, when I was wide-eyed and optimistic, the pastor said sin works on our hearts like nails in a tire. Subtle pricks that deflate one's faith over time. From the moment I heard that, I feared it was true. Now it was happening to me.

If I could name my nails, I'd call them uncertainty, disappointment, loneliness. When I felt them pierce me, I prayed God would remove their steel prongs. But he didn't, and all I could do was be angry. It was another blow from a father who wasn't a father. Where was he when the questions came? "Say something," I cried when the doubt-nails punctured my faith. I can't articulate the feeling, except to say a door had slammed shut, and I was alone in the dark.

I envisioned the church women I used to know, manicured hands interlocked in suburban chains of prayer. In the carpeted room across from the church gymnasium, we set our Starbucks cups on the round tables next to shiny Bibles and notebooks. Because we'd been taught to pray about everything, that God walked with us at all times, we petitioned him for car repairs, for better jobs, for speedy real estate transactions. We believed that when our kids were sick, he healed. When our luck was down, prayer was our rabbit's foot. I never stopped to ask why he'd heal my son's fever when mothers were burying their babies every day. Was God picking favorites? And if he had created all things, didn't that include the suffering as well as the cure? What kind of game was this? I wanted to know too much, and answers are antithetical to faith.

For many years, religion had been an anchor, but now it isn't strong enough to hold me. My soul is a paper ship, drifting in the current of the unknown.

***

Without religion, my internal world collapses and leaves me feeling deflated. I educate myself on the therapeutic nature of yoga, the mind-body connection and the spiritual components of the practice — elements I'd previously ignored while bending and twisting on my mat. Yoga engages me and teaches me to step into the moment and just be in that moment — to be present in my skin with the rhythm of my breath and the slow, steady beat of my heart. I learn to occupy myself in all the places religion had once lived. What is it like to be me, and who am I apart from everything I'd clung to: my marriage, the church, and the notion that God was my father? Yoga becomes an expedition, a journey to the depths of myself.

In tree pose, I stretch out my toes and take root, as I lengthen my spine and draw my hands up toward the sky. I am a mighty sequoia, strengthened by the wind. In lotus pose, I rest my palms on my knees and turn my attention lovingly inward. Each exhale feels like an emotional release. I no longer fumble through scriptures in search of meaning, plead for answers or strive for change. I tell myself I have what I need. And when I hear my voice, it sounds like the truth.

Precarious poses bring new challenges. While attempting tricky arm balances, I face plant again and again. Each failure unleashes a swarm of self-defeating thoughts. They sting and buzz at my ego, and I am forced to remember that tenacity drives away fear. I grow more determined with each fall. I begin to see my mat as a training ground for life. If I achieve balance here, I will feel more stable in the world. Equilibrium on the outside, equilibrium on the inside. Eventually, my arms strengthen and my gaze narrows. I find my drishti, the external point upon which I can fix my focus. My hands move mindlessly into position. My weight shifts, bones lock, breath flows like a steady current. Here I am, holding myself up in bakasana (crow pose) and it feels like actual flying.

Reaching a physical goal is an emotional win, and each one becomes a salve on my scars. Every movement is a metaphor. How far can I stretch, bend, move with fluidity and power? Building muscle and gaining flexibility is not merely a matter of the body, but of the spirit too.

At the end of a robust flow, my body sinks into the mat, into savasana, a still pose in which I find myself squarely in front of myself, like a child with her face against a window. I behold myself as never before. I close my eyes and see the state of my mind, the mayhem of too much thinking. Domestic thoughts hail-storm inside my head. *Did I remember to pay the electric bill, wash Sym's martial arts uniform, turn in the school forms for that field trip?* Then the existential crisis: *Am I a good mother, a good woman, a good writer, a good friend?* Then the guilt: *This is stupid. I'm wasting my morning. Shouldn't I be doing something else?* But there are pockets of silence too, warm and enveloping. I learn to surrender to these, and I feel something shifting in me. A sense of peace permeates the chaos and the hail storm melts into rain, into dew, into mere smudges of old worry on my consciousness. At last, I learn to conjure the calm from the corners of my mind, where fear and anxiety forced it down. I learn a new variation of prayer — gratitude.

Chapter 11

An Image Seared in My Memory

I have distance; I have space, and these things can be dangerous. With my marriage now far behind me, I begin to entertain ghosts — the ghosts of who we were. Memories come to haunt me. Sym was nearly three years old when I arrived home from work to find him red-faced and shirtless in the doorway. His tiny mouth trembled like a hummingbird's wings. J sat transfixed in front of the television. I bent down to face my child and found torment in his eyes. His sweet breath was hot and quick on my neck.

"What happened?" I asked. His little chest bore the faint imprints of a beating. The sight of it flipped my internal switch and rendered everything dark.

I'd heard that a person could steal your heart, but here's where the possession took place — this moment, his little hand in mine.

"Don't worry about it," J snapped.

I had seen J pound out windows, hurl furniture across the room, toss a holiday pie at the ceiling — the hot bits of sweet potato clinging overhead. His sharp glances could shrink me back like a turtle into its shell. But strange as it seemed, I'd never imagined he'd hurt our sons. This was a dreadful aberration, I reasoned. But more than a decade later, Sym recounted other cruel incidents in counseling sessions — the time his dad made him eat cat feces from the litter box as a punishment. For what, I didn't ask. It didn't matter.

J rarely turned his anger on KJ.

"It's because he looks just like him," my mother noted in a phone conversation one day. Not many people can stand to punch their own face.

Sym, however, boasts many of my genes — from the curve of his face to his creative tendencies. Nearing the end of our marriage, J cornered him and yelled so ferociously, Sym peed his pants on the spot, and I watched the urine trickle down like hot fear. The image is seared in my memory. If I could gather the dust of that day in my hands, I'd reshape the moments that caused my son pain.

***

All we need is Windex...

As a girl, I watch my mother burst into my bedroom. I see her mad form rushing toward me in threadbare pajamas. It's 5 a.m. or so but I'm not alarmed. I am accustomed to watching her scurry about as if the fire alarm has been pulled.

"Slide over," she commands, nudging me to the far end of my twin mattress.

She tugs at the fitted sheet and a corner springs free. She does this with the precision of a hotel maid, which she is not. But according to her, the entire family thinks so, which is why she vows to rent her own apartment and never give us her address. As with many of her fantasies, the plan never comes to fruition. Mom's actual employment involves computers and customer accounts. However, clean sheets, lemon-scented floor tiles and smudge-free glass are her specialties. Her compulsory cleaning habits do not strike me as obsessive. When I enter the house with grimy sneakers, I expect her to pop up like a wild-eyed jack-in-the-box, wielding a bottle of sanitizer. I assume this is standard Mom behavior, like spit-shining smudged faces or forcing broccoli on picky eaters. I am too young to know where the lines are drawn, but when a friend spends the night, I receive my first clue that something is amiss.

"What's happening?" My friend whispers into my pillow while shaking me awake. I hear the vacuum cleaner rumbling in the hallway as my mother curses at imaginary clutter. I rip off my pajamas and toss them on the floor where Mom will come to collect them like the groaning neighborhood waste truck.

"Laundry," I tell my confused friend before pulling my pillow overhead and drifting back to sleep.

***

When KJ is small and wobbly, J and I take him to a diner that serves breakfast all day. I snap on a white bib and wipe down the wooden high chair before corkscrewing my boy into his newly cleaned seat. J and I scan our menus and I consider the least messy options for KJ — scrambled eggs with fruit seem better than pancakes and syrup. Another set of parents and their toddler sit across the room near the window. Their child is about KJ's age. Pigtailed and plump, the girl chatters above the din of the crowded room. Armed with a fat plastic spoon, she smatters the table with applesauce like an artist indulging her muse. Her food-streaked cheeks are full and bright. No one wipes her face with napkins or plucks crumbs from her curls. I want this messiness, this freedom, for me, for my child. It's a strange thing to want.

I'm at a table with my son and a stack of napkins but mentally, I am back in my childhood bedroom. It's 5 a.m. and this time, I'm the one changing the sheets.

***

I am not my mother. I am not my mother, I tell myself as I sweep the floor, straighten a rumpled rug or pick lint off my sons' clothing. It is as though I am her in those moments, in method and mind. I cannot help but examine my hands to be sure they are my own.

As my boys grow up, I continue to scrutinize my behavior while fumbling through motherhood. I know that while I compare my mother's cleaning habits to mine and assess our parental failures, what I am really asking myself is this: Will I be stronger than she was? Will I make the mistakes she made? These questions have plagued me my entire life as my inner voice jeers *you're weak, you're flawed, you'll never be good enough.*

When Sym was 3 years old, he wandered from the backyard one afternoon while I assembled sandwiches in the kitchen. From the window, I could see him playing next to KJ, sprawled out on a wedge of grass behind our home with Hotwheels in his lap. I looked away for a second and when I glanced back out the window, he was gone. My little boy had vanished.

I sprinted around the yard then barreled into the alley where aluminum garbage cans shimmered in the sun, their dented, half-cocked lids exposing bulging trash bags. I searched the jagged hedges, the parked cars and open yards. I spotted a child's pink tricycle tipped on two fat wheels, a cracked garden gnome and a pair of rusted lawn chairs. Still no son.

I rushed about, looked left, right, left, right, as I hollered for my child. An earthquake had begun to rumble at my core, the vibrations of which traveled throughout my body. I continued my search, scanning, calling, scanning, calling. I visualized his outfit — green denim pants and a matching striped shirt. Would I have to recite these details to someone, some officer of the law? *My son is yea high; his hair is dark and curly.*

When I heard a car door slam, it sounded like a clanging cymbal in my ear. My senses had heightened to superhero proportions. I was ready to tip the world on its side. Hulk-mom. Eventually, I spotted him a few houses over, hunkered down on a picnic bench, thrusting his cars across the weathered wood.

Late at night, these parental blunders float to the surface of my thinking like dead things bobbing on a lake. I lost my child. He could've been kidnapped, could've been hit by a car, could've fallen into a well, like baby Jessica in Midland, Texas, 1987. Could've, could've, could've, and it would've been my fault. How many times will I fail to protect my sons?

***

I am working as a magazine staff writer when my aunt texts me on a Tuesday morning. *Read the advice column in the newspaper. It could be us.* A woman writes to Dear Annie, frustrated because her family won't face their demons. They have collective amnesia, she says. Collective amnesia — the phrase packs a punch to my gut. This is our disease, the disease of forgetting what we know, the compulsion to sweep the dirt under the rug. Later, I read an article in *Psychology Today*. Following a trauma, it's not unusual for the victims to be in denial. When children are abused, when a spouse cheats, when something unimaginable happens. But how far do we go in forgetting? I think about all the years I cooked and cleaned because it was all I could do to make a house a home. If I mopped the floor, could I erase the imprint of my husband's angry boots? If I wiped the table clean, could I forget his vile words over dinner?

And my mother — did she think a spritz of Windex could wipe the past clean? The right amount of elbow grease could polish a dirty conscience? Perhaps we are tidy by nature, genetically inclined to carry our mops and brooms. But maybe it's something more. I wonder if Mom thought clean sheets could undo the sins in the night, could usher us into sweet dreams.

Chapter 12

Love Him Hard

Some nights when I wrestle with sleep, I hear the metallic clunk of the ambulance door. It is a phantom sound that will haunt me forever, I think. The memory twitches to life like some monster in a low-budget horror flick: Sym sitting upright on a stretcher, foaming at the mouth, eyes floating in the darkness. We'd been fighting that evening, as per our routine. It always starts the same way. After hours of video game play, I find him feral, sweaty and cursing at the television or pounding on the desk where his gaming console blinks a red eye.

"Please shut it off now," I beg. "You've had enough."

"Get out of my room" he snarls and shoots his arm toward the door. The ceiling fan whirls above my head in his bedroom, where dented soda cans and a small army of food-crusted plates and bowls congregate. He will have to clean it all later, I think. But *later* unfolds a bit differently this night...

At 5'11", he has nine inches on me, and he uses them like chips on a poker table — always winning. His anger rattles my insides and I realize I fear my own son. But it's not him so much in these moments. Who it is, I can't say. He looks like the boy I know, only amplified and magnified. A dark comic book version.

Nudging me out of the way, he storms into the bathroom and locks the door.

"Just wait," he says. "You'll see." His words don't register until minutes later when he flings the door open again and I see a face I have not seen in a decade — his child face, features small and quivering, eyes muddled with panic.

"What did you do?" I screech.

Chlorine fumes hang sharp in the air as he crouches over and convulses, spewing tidal waves of bleach into the sink. I know what he did. I just can't believe he did it. I recall the video he showed me months prior.

"Mom, today is the anniversary of Amanda Todd's death," he'd said.

"I don't know who that is," I said as he stepped into my room and clicked on the lamp near my bed. I had been trying to sleep for an hour, but I welcomed those occasional night chats because they offered rare glimpses into his otherwise guarded world. He set his laptop on my bed and we watched the YouTube video in which a somber, 15-year-old girl used a series of flashcards to tell her story. Ostracized, bullied and even physically assaulted by her peers, the girl made her first suicide attempt by drinking bleach. Later she succeeded by way of hanging and her videos went viral. I watched the screen throw light on my son's cheeks. His eyes were screwed to the monitor. Screwed to the fact of suicide: Here today, gone tomorrow. A life like a gust of wind.

When Sym was in ninth grade, his class was reading the book *13 Reasons Why*, a novel about a bullied student who'd killed herself. Scorned teens had become household names after death. The internet romanticized their suicides, and it seemed the ultimate revenge to publicly shame the young tyrants who taunted you. No one at school had bullied Sym, and he had no desire to die. Instead he was desperate to interrupt his pain cycle, to trip his emotional breaker.

"You can't drink poison expecting your enemy to die," I told Sym. But it didn't stop him from trying only a few months later.

I know there is a darkness burrowing in his center like a worm in the heart of an apple. I would do anything to keep him from feeling it. I want to love him so hard the sheer force of it lifts him out of the pain. Can a mother love that hard?

***

After calling 911, I reach my mother and she rushes over. I don't ask, she just comes, and later I will think of the way she showed up, the way she sat beside me wordless with her hands in her lap. Nothing so say, but so much to offer. The presence of a mother who went numb and limp and deaf to the sounds of her children crying out in the night. And I don't know the body of her regrets, or whether she has skeletons or living organisms, things that can creep in her mom-soul. But if I think of the good, I find memories of her reaching out. Of her arranging stacks of quarters on the counter. "Don't forget your lunch money." Of her remembering every birthday and gifting all the best things: a sparkly sweater, a pair of shoes or diamond stud earrings. Of her on the phone leaving messages. "I haven't heard from you in a week. What's going on? I'm worried." So many sides to a story, angles to consider. Angles of a mother.

I see yet another side of her as she takes the passenger seat and we follow the ambulance to the emergency waiting room. I watch the other haggard and impatient visitors cough and blow into soggy tissues. It's Sunday night, quiet with the television flashing a sitcom on the wall and the occasional sound of the glass doors swishing open to let a smoker back in or out. Mom doesn't say a word. She's not a talker, a crier, a consoler in times of grief. But she is here, and it feels like enough. I'm anxious, tapping my foot on the floor. What is taking so long and why do I have to wait here?

The last time I'd been at this hospital was four years ago, just after the boys and I had moved to Florida. I'd found KJ doubled over in his bedroom with a stomach ache. "Too many pizza rolls," he moaned. But it was more than that and I knew it. His symptoms worsened and soon he was throwing up bile. It was a Sunday like this one, and we sat in this same waiting room for hours until they scanned his abdomen then whisked him away for an emergency appendectomy. Now I am back, staring at the same bleak walls and watching the red-blue glow of the ambulance lights flicker in the window beside me. I have another sick child, I try to tell myself as they pump Sym's stomach in another room. Another sick child, that's all.

***

Sym's bleach cocktail caused minor damage, including some esophageal scars. In my memory, I returned to the hospital again the following morning. And I can't be sure, but I think his wrist was cuffed to the bedrail and a staff member lingered outside his door. Suicide watch. These images are like pieces of an unworked puzzle in my brain, but I think I prefer them that way. The Starbucks Frappuccino I brought him is the only thing vivid in my mind. I set it down on the bedside table. He sneered in my direction and turned his gaze to the television where an episode of *Ghost Hunters* played. I sat there, motionless, watching the whipped cream sink into the coffee and ice. Sink, sink, sink. I could commiserate with that.

Sym spends several days in the hospital before being transferred to a psychiatric center. When I'm allowed to visit, I bring books, colored pencils and drawing paper — the only things permitted. I wait in the lobby for a tattooed woman with a jingling set of keys to walk me down to the adolescent ward. We squeak down stretches of polished linoleum. In my footsteps I hear the word "guilty" in two syllables. Guil-ty. Guil-ty. Guil-ty. All of this is my fault somehow. Isn't the mother always the culprit?

As if she hears my thoughts, the woman chimes in.

"Your son is a good kid," she says as we round a corner and pass a closed lunchroom. If by some miracle I forgot where I was, I might mistake the place for a school. An ordinary high school where my son could toss his textbooks in a locker, shoot hoops in a drafty gymnasium and shove down the hallway with other teens in hoodies and ripped jeans. But we are not at school. The bell won't be ringing at the end of the day and Sym will not be coming home.

"He's really participating," the woman adds as we head toward the nurse's desk. I nod and force a smile.

Sym has a new diagnosis: ODD — oppositional defiant disorder. This is medical jargon for "stubborn," I think. Also: bipolar disorder, and they've begun medicating him accordingly. This time, I consent.

If family history plays a role, he has both sides to contend with: J's and mine. After years of psychiatric difficulties, my mother would confess she heard voices. Sometimes they told her to cram the dog into the microwave, to bake the barking bastard. But Mom fared better on medication.

A slender young nurse reaches from behind the counter. She hands me a document to sign.

"He's over there," she motions.

Cartoons are playing on an old wall-mounted television in the corner of the room. A glass window and a half-wall separate the space between the nurses' station and the visiting area. Construction paper artwork hangs on another wall, streaked with watercolors and curling at the edges. Sym sits in a plastic chair wearing clothes I've never seen. Standard issue shorts and a T-shirt. Gone are the days when this mother can dress her son, her child.

His elbows rest on his knees. When he sees me, he hops to his feet and roars. "Get out of here. I hate you. Get out."

I am a stray dog in an alley, a wretched, mangy mutt. Sym's face is aflame with emotion: fury, hatred, rage. I stand there, singed by the heat of him. The tattooed woman rushes in.

"You have to leave now," she says, reaching for my arm.

"No," Sym begs. "No." I watch him soften and drop into his chair. His eyes fill with tears and his three-year-old face emerges like a pearl in the oyster shell of his features. The file of him flies opens in my mind as if a storm has taken it. I watch the pages of my son flutter by: He is on my hip in the church hall, sweaty, teary, fussy. He is on his belly in the kitchen, pushing toy cars. *Vroom vroom.* He is on his bike in the late afternoon, pedaling, pedaling, pedaling away until the sun swallows him in a blaze. In the plastic chair, in the foreign clothes, in this place that isn't home, I understand that while he does not want me, a bigger part of my son still desperately needs me. Years later, I read about an addict who lashed out at her mother during a visit to the treatment facility.

"We can't stand seeing our mothers," she said. "They remind us of everything we did wrong; they make us feel guilty."

***

When Sym is back home, we start counseling again. Twice a month and as needed, we see a therapist whom Sym respects.

She wears an Afro and pink lipstick, which is striking against her dark skin. Her high-heeled shoes clack confidently against the tiles. She issues her directives in a smooth tone in her cramped office on a Thursday.

"Let's set some boundaries," she says. Sunlight from the open blinds paints gold stripes around the room. I sit next to Sym wearing a silky new blouse but feeling totally naked. Can't everyone see the *me* behind the threads, the mom-mess buried beneath?

"I'm a codependent parent and all of this is my fault," I imagine saying to clear the air. But I don't, and so we talk about limiting his gameplay and imposing some actual rules. I explain that his temper is so explosive, common-sense parenting seems impossible for me. I can assert the rules only until his anger leaps into high gear. After that, I hold on for the rough, jarring ride.

***

When medication makes him a blowfish, he feels better but doesn't care for the pudgy boy he sees in the mirror. He is 20 pounds up and decides to make a change. For years, I'd been asking Sym to run with me. I took the path across the street and followed it until the sidewalk ended. These are my sacred, sweaty rituals in which I streak through the night, endorphins surging. The black sky arches overhead and the streetlamps stamp my passage like gold stars on a progress report.

One evening, Sym joins me. At first, he is slow and he shuffles beside me, tennis shoes dropping on the concrete like bricks. Up, down, up, down. Every step a momentous effort. But night after night, he gains speed and I am surprised he's stuck with it. In those moments, I see glimmers of his childhood tenacity, of the time he plunked down beside me with my tennis shoes and said, "Teach me to tie them, Mom." His own shoes had Velcro straps, but he didn't care. We spent hours twirling the laces around, and he didn't give up until he could fasten a bow, flaccid as it was. Then there was the time he vowed to learn cursive, though it was no longer a requirement in school. He liked the loops and curves and came to me with a sheet of lined paper and a pencil. "Teach me," he said. And there went my afternoon.

Now he exercises regularly. He sold his video game system all on his own. He'd had enough. He does sit-ups in his bedroom and watches YouTube videos to learn the proper way to deadlift, squat, perform an overhead press. He adds morning runs to his regimen. From the window, I watch him make his way down the path in ragged gym shorts. He is upright and gliding. The sun blooms all around him, a carnation in the sky. I know it is hot and hard, and he is nearing the spot where the sidewalk slopes upward and gravity wages war with leg muscles. I remember the burning sensation as I watch him take his steps, not slowing or showing signs of strain. My son is strong now. I can't believe how strong.

***

His shoulders are round as melons and he relishes his physical achievements. "I hit a PR at the gym today," he tells me.

"PR?"

"Personal record, Mom." He kneels down beside me and I set down my book. I watch his mouth move as he describes his routine, spouts off his stats. "I lifted 545 on a conventional deadlift."

"That's incredible," I say. I feign amazement although I have no idea what this actually means. But I continue to ask questions, to reel him in so I can keep him close.

He demonstrates: hips forward, knees bent, grips the imaginary bar. I see the calluses on his hands, and I think of the day he stole my heart, the way it embedded in his palm like a fossil pressed to a stone. He's held it all these years. He holds it still.

Chapter 13

One Sure Thing

I buy a colossal cake cookbook with glossy photos of cherry-topped chocolate cakes, pudding-filled layered cakes and cakes with interesting names: snow skin mooncake and rum baba. I select a new cake to bake every week, poring over photos and essential steps. Which pan will I use: rectangular, circular, Bundt? I focus on ingredients, make a list of what I need: crushed pineapple, cream of tartar, almond extract. Then come the rituals — cracking the eggs in old familiar bowls, stirring the vanilla-laced mixture until the lumps of flour break free. The oven warming, the greased pan waiting. I feel domestic in my tiny kitchen with sticky hands and a counter snowed with flour.

I am not a highly skilled baker, but this feels right somehow. It's therapy, art, a canvas for the soul. I pour the batter, watch it spill out in gooey ribbons. It is two cups sugar, a quarter teaspoon of salt and so on. Everything measured, everything mixed. Bake at 300 degrees. I like to follow the recipe to get the outcome I expected. This is a sure thing. It's not like life at all, like pouring everything you had into a marriage and ending up divorced anyway, or praying for your child to be well then watching him claw through a room, enraged.

I bake because I feel something when I slide my hands into fluffy oven mitts and pull the cake from the metal rack. The hot blast of air on my skin and something else too, something maternal. I bake, therefore I am … what exactly I don't quite know. Perhaps I am the mother I want to be, if only for a moment. I am June Cleaver, Marion Cunningham, Carol Brady. I am not a single mom struggling to make ends meet, that mom with the messy hair, that mom who forgot to sign the school forms, who never showed up for parents' day, who cried through a box of tissues, a box of chocolates, a box of tissues again.

When I don my apron, it is a superhero's cape. I am the mother who fills her kitchen with the aroma of warm cake, who expertly slices two pieces and slides them on glass plates. One for each boy. When I call out "cake" and they hurtle in, eyes lit and hands swooping in for their share, I am the mother who is loved. And this is a sure thing.

***

It's 2014 and I've been divorced since 2005. The boys are stable, happy. They have jobs, girls, iPhones. The trifecta. When I think about all the time that's passed since we picked up and moved to Florida, I'm astounded. *What the hell have I been doing?* Reading books, baking cakes, exploring my yoga mat. I sit for long stretches in front of the mirror, examining my own face, every line and pore. I'm an archaeologist who has dusted off the rock and soil of heartbreak. I've collected the data, excavated the woman buried beneath the wreckage.

Meeting Mani awakened my heart and aroused my desire for love. He was someone who took an interest in me, who bought the books I was reading so we could discover the same stories in unison. He wondered what I was eating at the exact time I was sitting down to a meal. He'd imagined me at the table spooning oatmeal into my mouth the way you daydream about anything ethereal. The days before I'd met Mani were mundane. I was a mediocre mom with a black-and-white life. No one stopped to look. But Mani marveled, and his fascination with me was contagious. I saw myself through him and became quite enamored. *My life is colorful,* I thought. *I am colorful.* He gave me the courage to pursue love again, the will to want it and even expect it.

I'm in the living room now, with a notepad on my lap and the end of a pen in my teeth. I don't know if I am manifesting a good man or merely scribbling down adjectives. "You have to know what you want before you go looking," a friend said. It made sense. So I'm making a list of important qualities in a mate, now that I'm ready to date— on the internet that is. Online dating seems my safest option. My keyboard makes the intros. One step removed is where I want to be right now, where I feel steady enough to man-shop for a guy who might want an out-of-practice woman looking for a reason to shave her legs midwinter.

When I sit down to write my list, I am optimistic albeit nervous. I write "gentle, hardworking, humorous, kind." I'm almost opposed to pretty faces because some part of me sees this as a trap, as my past. Fool me once and you know how that went. But I realize I'm already making judgments. I should let this stuff go. I decide I'd like a friendly face. A fit type so we can hike and bike and run from the law (in theory of course). Bonnie and Clyde with real jobs.

With nervous hands, I post my photo and type up my profile. I'm 36, divorced, looking for a long-term companion. The next day, the emails hit my inbox. He's full of it, I say about this guy and that one. I examine profiles and nothing makes my heart leap. Is there supposed to be some heart leaping? I don't know how this is supposed to go.

"I feel like a dog with a bad nose," I tell a friend on the phone. "I'm just sniffing at everything."

"Go on some dates," she says. "You're making excuses not to get out there."

It's Saturday night. I'm standing in the living room, watching cars thunder down the road behind my house. Everyone is going somewhere while I scan the room for my slippers and the television remote.

A Date

Wes is one of four guys I decide to date. The best of the bunch, turns out. One smelled like booze on a Sunday morning and Mr. Law Degree wanted to know why I hadn't gone to a better college. I really could have been somebody, apparently.

Wes is early and I'm on time, so the waitress shows me to a booth near the window, where he's sitting with a colossal smile. There's sunlight on my side of the booth. I set down my purse then sit. I feel like a new penny plunking myself into a fountain, wishing all the way down. But not for magic or miracles, just something good. Some laughter and fun without painful stretches of silence in which someone cracks their knuckles to release the tension.

Harry's is a New-Orleans-style restaurant, a crusty brick building with a neon sign that lights up historic downtown like a disco ball at night. The windows are wide as walls so you can sip your beer and spy on the whole street: girlfriends teetering in stilettos, couples flashing date-night smiles. I have always enjoyed the vibe here. And the fried Oreos with chocolate sauce, which I shared with a friend on New Year's Eve. We clinked glasses of white wine, licked our sticky fingers clean as if it were symbolic. Fresh start. Clean slate.

Now Wes and I are on our second date. Our first date was a blur. It was last week, and we sat at a different restaurant where TVs beamed from above. I watched the monitors as if I gave a damn about motorcycle racing and sports commentary. It was an easy place to put my eyes in between nervous talk about work and who knows what. I can't recall the details, only that I didn't spill a drink or stumble on my own feet when I stood up. I half-hugged him when we left, a one-arm deal that I found out later he didn't care for because it made him feel like someone's creepy uncle. When we learn each other, he will understand that my affections show up elsewhere. Not in hugs or kisses but maybe in batches of double fudge brownies and other domestic favors.

I'm less nervous now, at Harry's. The waitress brings a basket of bread and our drinks. I watch Wes take the stack of plates and separate them. One, two. He quickly removes a wedge of warm bread and begins to slather it with butter. We're talking about something, but I don't know what because the bread is all I can think about. This hunk of baked dough is going to tell me more than he can say. I think about what my sister said to me when we were teens. "You're one of the good ones." She smiled, scooted inside and shut the car door behind her. We were in a parking lot somewhere and I was in the passenger seat. I had leaned over to pop the lock on her door so she didn't have to fumble with her keys.

"I'm confused," I said.

She revved the engine on the little blue Ford she'd later blow up for lack of oil. "If you pay attention, you can tell who the good ones are," she said.

I'm paying attention now. The knife roams across the bread as he chats. He sets down the slice and clears his throat, slides the plate across the table in front of me and gets to work on a piece for himself. First me, then him —this is the order of things, and it's never just bread and butter.

***

We've been texting and emailing, texting and emailing like modern-day pen pals. He sends pics of sunrises in the morning. *Rise and shine.* We go on dates every week. He sends me his address and I drive to his house on a Saturday. We sit for a while on the sofa. I brought lawn chairs for the drive-in theater, a package of pistachios and a bag of heart-shaped chocolates. He has a bottle of Reisling and a few plastic wine glasses.

"We should leave in about 15 minutes," he says. I nod, look around at the white walls, black drapes and ordinary everything. When I ask, he points me to a bathroom down the hall. It's white-tiled and sterile. There are no drippy bottles of shampoo in the shower or lumpy washcloths in a wad. No shaving cream splatter on the mirror or rumpled towels on the rack. Everything is pristine and for some reason, it's unsettling. *This is not a bachelor's home,* I think. I take a seat on the toilet lid and scan the garbage can at my side. It's empty, lined with a plastic bag. If I could find a few dirty cotton swabs or maybe a clod of dried toothpaste in the sink, I'd feel better. *Look,* I'd say, *he's not too good to be true.*

In the garage, we load up his car. The trunk is open and he's arranging the lawn chairs inside. "Anything else we should bring? Bug spray?"

"Yes, please," I say. "There's something about me they love. I'm bug bait." He chuckles and goes back inside. As I stand near the lip of the trunk, I notice red speckles on the cement near my feet. I lean in, examine it. It's probably paint, but it could be a bloodstain. I search the garage for potential clues. Weapons. I see a storage rack against the wall, loaded with greasy rags and garden shears, dog-eared rolls of duct tape. A red toolbox, gleaming. I'm replaying CSI episodes in my head. Ten minutes ago he was Mr. Perfect and now he could be a serial killer. I don't think he keeps a lunchbox full of panties, but perhaps he has a closet full of skulls. He enters the garage again and his green eyes are soft as summer grass. He hands me the bug spray and we're back on track.

We don't watch a smidge of the movie. Inside the car, we chat and laugh until we decide to step outside and set up our chairs, alternately gazing at the screen, the sky, the screen, the sky again. It's a strange thing to see the techno glow of Hollywood faces against the dusky drape of night, the juxtaposition of technology and nature.

Wes reaches over and opens his palm. I pluck out three fat pistachios and pop them into my mouth. He tops off my wine and I hold it up, let the liquid kiss my lips before it slides down. After sitting a while, Wes stands up, shakes out and moves over to the car. I follow, lean against the hood and watch kids skip-run to the concession building, dollar bills flapping in their hands. A low-slung moon offers a pearly smile from beyond the massive screen we're not watching. I smell popcorn and see a gaggle of kids hurtling toward a pickup truck, dropping kernels as bright as dandelion heads in the dusty gravel lot. After they pass, there is nothing but Wes and the tepid July air and I try to remember the grinning moon as I close my eyes and feel his lips press into mine. Tonight, I am a little fish, swimming in the big of everything, of the dazzling screen and sky and this date that doesn't suck. Swept up in the tide of possibilities: of me with a man who can love without rage. Is he that man? He looks at me with eyes wet with oceans. And I swim.

***

This is love...

I'm standing near a chain link fence outside daycare - or maybe it's preschool - my little hands pressed against the warm metal. I'm watching the cars materialize in the lot, rumble into the carpool lane then squeak to a stop. Doors fly open and parents wave to the teacher, who is stationed like a flagpole amid an army of students. One or two kids break free from the crowd and skip to the car. Another car pulls up and this one isn't mine either. My hands are sweaty, and they slip off the fence then drop to my sides, limp as doll arms.

Where are they, where are they, where are they? I'm desperate for the golden whale, the Mercury Grand Marquis my grandpa maneuvers same as his massive sled dog named Egor — dramatically, lurchingly. The car is boxy and long, the color of brass with plush interior and a polished grille that glistens in the sun. When I climb in, I will click my seatbelt into place and smell my grandma's perfume. The radio will be playing AM 920, The Carpenters *We've Only Just Begun* or something by Sinatra. I will exhale and reset.

These people are warm and safe. Grandpa wields fists full of peppermints and butterscotch discs. "Which hand?" he prods, then fakes amazement when I choose the right one. Somehow I always do.

Grandpa wears baseball caps with crepe paper poppies twisted around the strap in remembrance of the soldiers he won't speak about, the war that's locked in his memory. A row of curls loop around the base of his hat in soft silver chunks. His friends call him Curly, a name my grandmother hates since curly is also a pet name assigned to bald men, same as cueball. Grandma refers to him as Arthur. "Oh Arthur," she says with scorn when she spies his threadbare socks.

"They're my church socks," he mocks. "They're holy." This makes me laugh. In fact, mostly everything he does makes me laugh. And he couldn't be prouder when I do.

For all his playfulness, Grandma will return the same scornful headshake, tone, phrase, "For God's sake, Arthur." She won't crack a smile when he teases or laughs but even I will know that it's there. Like the sleeping sun beneath a clot of gray clouds, her amusement remains out of sight. But it's there. It is, like their mutual love and admiration of one another, always, always there. It's a palpable love, the kind that can anchor a heart. The kind that sends my internal clock ticking, counting the hours, minutes, seconds until I can hop in the backseat again, click on my seatbelt, smell her perfume. And the Carpenters will play on the radio, or maybe Sinatra. *I Get a Kick out of You.*

As we idle at a stoplight, Grandpa will beam as the lyrics catch up with his chorus. He will turn to Grandma and croon with Old Blue Eyes, "I get a kick out of you," thrusting out the "you" then holding it in his palm like a gift between them. I will almost see it shimmering there like some tangible thing, a tiny diamond or a foil-wrapped chocolate morsel.

Looking back, I realize this memory is a part of me, a thread sewn into my heart. After love ravaged me, I dare to say it was the thread that kept my heart from ripping clear out of my chest. *Love is possible,* I think. *And I, as much as anyone, deserve it.*

***

I'm wearing a pink cotton dress and a smile that feels like someone else's. When I see the photo we took on this day, I remember the nerves. I sit at a table with Wes's family. We're at a restaurant on the beach and the air is a salty vapor. I order smoked fish dip and crackers, then set down my menu and gaze at the rickety pier and the boats streaking in the distance, leaving frothy trails in their wake. My hands in my lap, my self on display. I wonder what they think of me and damn this wind, which keeps flinging tufts of hair into my mouth, eyes, nose. Every orifice is under attack and I am fighting with my own ridiculous mane. Wes puts his arm on my shoulder to both comfort me and showcase my quality. Every so often his face turns to mine and he sings me a song with his eyes. It floats between us and drowns out the sounds of silverware and small-talk. As the years pass, his family will become my family. When we visit, they'll teach me how to give and receive hugs. They'll pour me red wine and say, "I have a nice piece of salmon for you." On summer weekends, we'll go on beach vacations with them and meet up early on the sand to take long walks before breakfast. On Christmas Eve, we will pile wrapped gifts in front of his mother's fireplace and then pass them around after the meal. I will find a little box in my lap that contains a silver engraved bracelet. When I hold it up to the light, I'll choke down tears as I read: *Be you, love you, all ways, always* — a gift from Wes's adult daughter.

***

It's Wes's turn to meet my family — the boys. Sym does just fine. He's friendly, even offers the kind of handshake you'd give at a job interview. He stands up straight like he does in his martial arts class, when his voice booms with a "Yes, ma'am" for his sensei. I'm glad to see he didn't bury his manners behind cutting glances and layers of sarcasm. He is 15 and impressed with Wes's car. He immediately Googles the model to learn the value and then sits on the sofa with his phone in his palm, skimming car sites and looking glazed. In exactly a year, he'll have his turn behind the wheel. I'll behave like a cat being bathed, screeching and pawing at the dashboard, so Wes will be the instructor who ultimately teaches Sym to drive. In my humble Kia Spectra, the two will navigate the city, Wes patiently prodding, "Let's try that 3-point-turn again. You ready?"

KJ is less eager to meet Wes. He told me he'd behave but he's not making good so far. We're at a Denny's in Orlando and Wes has booked us all a hotel so we can hang out and be tourists in our own state. We have a helicopter ride planned and maybe we'll swim, shop, sleep late and eat omelets tomorrow morning. Right now, we're perusing our menus and I'm on high alert. KJ is loud and wide-eyed, a picnic fly at the table. He takes sips of his water and slams it down. I try to fill the silence with chatter but KJ interjects. It's as if he's been waiting to say this, saving the seed for just the right time to plant it. He looks directly at Wes. "What are your intentions for my mom?"

This is more a challenge than a question and Wes finds it slightly humorous. KJ leans forward, arms latched across his chest, awaiting some retort.

Wes laughs. Sym laughs nervously, an attempt at adding levity. I signal to the waitress, "Please... we're ready to order."

When the food comes, KJ slings insults in between bites as we eat. Wes is unfazed.

In the car, KJ says Wes is bad with directions. "My dad never gets lost," he snorts as we weave through traffic toward our hotel. I turn my face to the window and consider banging my head on the glass. Hard. Again and again.

I watch Sym text a friend at the hotel: My brother is a jerk. I can't believe my brother.

***

A lot has happened, and nothing has happened. KJ is 20 now and we are having dinner at a table in our new home. I am looking out at the backyard where green vines have sprung up along the fence and oak trees sway like dancing women. Wes sits at the head of the table and KJ is our guest. Our frequent guest. He lives across town in a little house he shares with his new wife, Anna, who works third shift at the hospital. But twice a week or more I see him standing on the hooked rug near the door, keys jingling in his hand.

"You making dinner?" he asks. "Smells like something…" His nose shoots up like an antenna.

"Why don't you move in, KJ?" Wes calls from the sofa.

"Hell no," I say. "I can't tolerate those feet."

Everyone laughs, moves to the kitchen to pour drinks and pile food on our plates.

At the table now, I wonder how we got here. There were no great debates or interventions, extravagant plans or schemes I invented to get my men to play nice. No books or blogs read on the topic of blending the family. Just momentum. Boxes in and boxes out; dinners cooked and consumed. And it was not at all like when KJ was 5 and I held up a loaded fork pleading, "You'll love this if you just try it."

***

Expanding the family…

It's been five years since we lost our little dog Carlo to Rudy. Christmas is approaching, and I decide I need something special this year. I need a dog.

"If you want a dog, let's get a dog," Wes says one Saturday afternoon.

Wes has seen me gawk at mutts on the street. He's heard me baby-talk to excited beasts in the tone mothers use on their blushing infants and wobbling toddlers. Carlo had taught me to treasure the sweet serenade of dog yelps upon arriving home. I thought how happy Wes and I were with each other, with all our domestic rituals: tickling each other's feet while watching nighttime television, lying on beach towels in the backyard, the warm sun thick as honey on our skin. So happy we are, and yet we could be happier still. Happier with a dog.

I understand there are two kinds of people in the world: those who love dogs and those who simply haven't met the right ones. Wes is stuck in the latter group. It's not his fault. His time has not yet come, so of course he has preconceived notions, territorial rules and non-negotiable terms. Silly man.

"No dogs on the bed," he declares as we work out the details of our plan. "And the couch is off limits too. I don't want to walk around with pet hair all over my clothes."

"Of course," I assure him as I conjure memories of Carlo on the couch, Carlo on the bed, Carlo on a dining room chair, one wily paw on the table, ready to stake his claim. I see no reason to debate my views with Wes. There are things he simply can't understand, having never experienced true dog love. Explaining these grand and glorious mysteries now will only confuse my poor man.

We spend a week scouring adoption sites in search of the perfect pup: a small breed, a Carlo clone. I land on a scruffy contender named Snoopy, a wiry-haired weirdo with a Tina-Turner style hairdo that is comical and endearing. But when we show up at the shelter, he is no longer available.

"What now?" Wes asks. Later he confesses he was relieved. Snoopy didn't strike him as the pickup-truck-riding type or the kind that would spook an intruder— not that we were in the market for a security system. But it is a perk he's considered.

Snoopy aside, we observe the other dogs vying for adoption, the howling faces of labradors, hounds and terriers. The groaning gets wilder and more desperate as the tour commences. I hone in on all the droopy eyes and flaccid tongues. The cages rattle as dogs hop up, bark and pace. The smell of dingy fur and mud-pawed holes billows in the yard. Wet noses worm through fence holes as we pass. Which nose is ours? Each seems decent enough in terms of size, shape and sniffability. And then I see it. The mutt of my dreams, the cherub of pit bulls, pink-bellied with a dancing tail and ears like crisp white teepees. She watches me. Her eyes are pleading domes, black as a shade of grief. Her gaze is voodoo, and I know instantly she is ours. I know the way you know anything profound — with a tingle and an ache. I think for a moment she could be my Carlo reincarnated, but in reality she could clean her teeth with Carlo. Still, I sense she is gentle and loving and perfectly equipped to teach us to aspire to unconditional love, which is the duty and role of all dogs. When the handler unlatches her pen, we slip inside the cement square. The 50-pound babe bounds toward me, jowls slapping against her teeth. I bend down and she puts a paw on my knee, her tongue on my face and works it up and down like a painter glazing the canvas.

"Oh my! Someone made a friend," the handler says as she tugs on the dog's collar. "This is Lady."

Lady: Bull-legged, beefy-necked and drooling. Hardly a lady.

"I *need* her," I say.

After Lady is vet-checked, microchipped and deemed suitable for adoption, we rescue her from the pound. She seems to know this fact. When she scurries to the truck, Wes hoists her onto the leather seat in front of the window and the shelter fades to memory as her new life clicks into view like a colorful View-Master reel. With his cell phone, Wes records her elated face. Later, I will watch it and think how foreign she was to us then, like a postcard or a photograph of some place we'd yet to go.

"Lady" becomes "Mia Sophia," and a few weeks later we tack on "Princess," making her "Princess Mia Sophia," a title she easily earns. We buy her an engraved collar that bears her new name (pink with tiny hearts), and as we get to know our girl, our collection of names for her grows. Wes calls her "Bug," as in "Lady Bug." When she is nose-deep in hibiscus or skulking near the fence, he wails, "Bug-Bug," while patting his thighs to entice her. Upon hearing it, her ears flip up like wild puppets and she barrels toward the sound of his voice — oafish and slap-happy, a pig at the sound of "Sooey."

***

Some women use their wiles. I can't say what spell Princess Mia brews on a Saturday afternoon while I grocery shop. The house is quiet when I return and what I see is this: limbs flung on a mattress, two chests heaving, one pillow puckering between the faces of my dog and man. I stand there for a moment and listen to Wes and Mia breathe in unison. They are nose to nose, taking a long, delicious nap. The first of many together. *No dogs on the bed,* I think, smiling. He's been voo-dooed.

But there are things we didn't know about our Mia. Storms set her off. Separation makes her anxious. Wes and I come home one afternoon to a splintered door frame and a closet door ripped clean from the hinges. As thunder roars outside and lightning flickers at the windows, we navigate the minefield of gnawed wood in the hallway leading to the bedroom.

"Bug-Bug," Wes calls as we give each other astounded looks and make slow-motion gestures — pointing in silence at a blood-streaked wall, mouths wide. Inside the spare bedroom, we flip on the light and find our girl trembling beneath a heap of wet blankets, stinking of urine. It is the first of many storm-fueled outbursts. During other storms, Mia proceeds to rip down two more door frames, mangle her wire pet crate into modern art, and chew, claw or eviscerate various objects.

On New Year's Eve, fireworks crackle and pop outside our bedroom. With a few Rieslings and a cheese platter weighing us down, Wes and I crawl into bed and fall asleep. But the neighborhood gets lively and sometime before midnight, a paw appears on our bed. Then a panting snout. With one eye shut, I see her frenzied face with every snap and burst of a firecracker. Her breathing intensifies and soon she is on our bed, pawing at our throats as if she could climb inside us. I bear-hug her, but with every new explosion she spirals. She circles the bed like a crazed wolf.

"This is too much," I say. "What are we going to do?"

Without a word, Wes sits up, grabs his pillow and leads Mia into the closet where he coaxes her to the floor and shuts the door. I lie in bed and watch the colors splatter the sky: orange, green, red. They pop and splinter, particles fading to nothing. At some point my eyes shut and we sleep all night, Mia and Wes in the stifling closet, me on our king-sized bed. When I wake up the following morning, I think how I love that man, how I love our life, our family.

***

Dogs make you do things you *should* do but probably wouldn't had they not insisted. Since we adopted Mia, we have taken her for countless walks — in the early mornings when the dew clings to the grass and the whole neighborhood is fragrant. At night when we'd rather be watching television but discover instead there is a marvelous moon, a diamond in the black boundless sky. Walking a dog is not so much a chore as a privilege — the ritual of watching her head cock at the mention of a walk, the tap-dance of her paws as she rushes to the door, beaming. However long she takes to sniff the weathered mailbox posts or meander up the street, it is never too long. More than a physical exercise, it's a discipline. How far can we stray from our phones, laptops, never-ending lists? Together, we learn to step away and admire the deep purple flowers crowning the crape myrtle branches.

Chapter 14

Petals of Rain

Drip

I am a twenty-something mother of two when KJ starts school. He meanders onto the playground and into the whirling sea of child-monsters who are yelping and leaping on the concrete in front of the building. I am having one of those slow-motion moments in which a data file of emotions — heartbreak, fear and anxiety — downloads into my consciousness. I feel it all sink in as I see his small body, sporting new jeans and a collared shirt, swimming in the bulk of his backpack. He is going somewhere I cannot go. I feel my hand squeeze his a little tighter. I watch him pull free and march away like a battery-operated toy. I'd stocked his cartoon backpack with all of the requisite items: 2-ply Kleenex, a pack of sharpened pencils, wide-ruled paper, Elmer's glue, a box of jumbo crayons and all of the other essentials on the kindergarten list. But these things are not enough.

Panic sits in my throat and I consider taking him home, walking him right back to our house where he belongs because he is not ready for school. But I know the truth is that he is plenty ready — and I am not. I hadn't anticipated it being so hard, had not imagined I would be one of those nervous moms. I am an off-brand diaper mom, a cereal-for-dinner mom. Somehow a sharp prong of fear has perforated my sanity and strung me up like a largemouth bass.

I stand on the playground watching him. The bell rings and he looks back for a moment, his eyes salute their goodbyes.

Sym and I walk home, his pudgy legs stomping on the sidewalk because he is a boy who insists on doing everything hard, hammer-like. He is three years old and soon he will leave me too. He will march away and not look back, a kindergarten robot ready to assert his independence. Tears come and the sky begins to bellow. We have several blocks left till home, and I feel a cool cascade of rain. In an instant, we are saturated, slogging our limp jeans and waterlogged tennis shoes down the street. My little boy squeals, shoots his hands in the air and says, "Run, Mom."

"No baby," I say. "Let's go slow."

Drop

We're lost. I have seen the same yellow mailbox three times, which means we are driving in circles. I am in the passenger's seat of my new friend's Toyota. We have taken a day trip to a wildlife park not far from my new home in Florida. I'm divorced now, raising my sons solo in a little house on a modest street. This coworker of mine has become a good friend, one of the few friends with which I share secrets over strong cups of coffee and pão de queijo — Brazilian cheese bread. She is from Brazil, an older woman with a charming accent and a modern hairstyle. She always hugs me when she sees me, leaving the warm imprint of her perfume on my skin like a flower petal pressed between the pages of a book — a cherished keepsake. It lingers on my blouse like the ghost of Coco Chanel. We are exhausted now, having spent the whole day watching snakes shed their skins and ducks flitter their wings in the sun-tinged pond at the park. She has captured it all from a zillion different angles with her smartphone. She is one of those photo-obsessed people who makes you pose with your glass raised, pose with your hip cocked against an enormous cypress tree, pose as the sun melts over the landscape. I am posed out. My feet hurt and a damp blast of cool air is pounding me from the air vents. We are lost, hours from home, hungry and grimy.

"Pull over," I tell her. "Let's figure this out."

She does. We fuss with the maps on our phones for a moment before we pull off in the right direction — finally. I lean back into my seat, untangle a clump of wind-mangled curls.

"We will be home by 7, my friend," she says in a singsong voice.

Her words still hang in the air when the mouth of the sky groans and spews a hard, heavy rain. The road is awash with it, and we struggle to see anything but the bug-eyed glow of other headlights. We may very well be driving into a cave or off a cliff. We coast until we see the low gleam of a BP sign and an empty lot beckoning. It does not rain like this in Wisconsin, like the sky is an angry ocean, spilling its salty wet fury. My friend slams the car into park, and we sit for a moment, watching the wiper blades whisk back and forth in a futile attempt to clear the swampy windshield. She looks at me and we both exhale as if we are overfilled balloons, ready to burst. I laugh a helpless high-pitched laugh, and then we laugh together until our bellies cramp and our eyes are slick with tears. The rain thumps the car and a delicate ribbon of my friend's perfume dances all over my senses and sparkles like a promise in the dark.

Drip

They say the squeaky wheel gets the grease. He's not the squeaky one. In fact, he is almost silent as he moves through the dark house on weekend mornings, wearing his white Polo and black bowtie, fastening his apron before work at his first job — a dietary aide for the elderly.

When people tell me what a great server he is, how he pours the coffee with such patience and handles the enormous food trays with ease, I smile. They tell me I raised a good boy but it's hard to accept the praise. "KJ is self-sufficient," I say. Had he been my only child, I might have become a smug mom, doling out parenting advice to mothers with feisty kids: *Here's what I do when such and such happens. Works like a charm.*

I never have to field phone calls from angry teachers on his behalf or worry he is not where he said he'd be. I ache with the knowledge that KJ deserves more than he gets from me. More attention, less pressure to be the household referee, to swoop in and bench his angry brother who refuses to play by the rules. He is the easy-button boy and I am glad because I spend all my energy on Sym.

It isn't much, but we have our carefree nights. Sometimes we explore the neighborhood roads. The boys ride scooters as I walk behind them with Carlo on the leash, tasting the sultry summer air. A symphony of insects echoes in the forests all around. "Try it Mom," KJ says, breathless, handing me his scooter. I take my turn down the dark hill, feeling the thrill of speed and wind and gravity working like a wing to sweep me into the night.

Later, we sprawl out in front of the television: KJ with his fruit punch in a glass and me with my enormous faux fur blanket. We watch seasons of *Lost* and *Parenthood* and *The Office*, and we laugh like friends at a sleepover. These are our moments, lovely as little flowers in the cracked cement of the day. But these nights lessen as Sym's outbursts increase.

Then comes our breakfast goodbye. I sit across from KJ at a cafe and he tells me he misses his friends, his life in Wisconsin. He is 17 and he's going back, he arranged it with his dad. Going back. Back in time? I know this is what he means. Is it his childhood he yearns for? Our family before the break? Trips to the corner candy store with his best bud Damon? I want to tell him he can't go back. All we can do is move forward, but I see that his mind is made up. I sip my ice water knowing he will return to Wisconsin and find that the old path no longer bears his footprints. Friends have moved on and even his father has forged a new life. "Here's your sister," J announces. "She's 3-years old."

But two years later and with more facial hair and a deeper voice, KJ comes home and it isn't a shock. I stand in the driveway and watch the sky change. I think of the word *Winterization* - a word I learned in grade school. When the season changes, it triggers hormones and chemicals that tell the trees to let go of their leaves. It's essential to the tree's survival. Letting go. But new leaves always grow in the spring. Radiant, rich and bright. My son has come home, winterized. And today we relish a new season.

Drop

At 37, I'm flying for the first time — Punta Cana.

"Is this going to be like La Bamba?" I ask Wes as we stuff sandals into our suitcase. He doesn't answer. I can see he's got a spreadsheet open in his head. It's what he does — Mr. Organization. I keep talking.

"You know, like Ritchie Valens... died in a plane crash?" He's choosing T-shirts now and folding them. "Ugh. I can't believe you never saw the movie." I fake outrage then break into a terrible rendition of the song *"La Bamba."* Wes joins in. *Ba-ba-bamba.*

At the airport, I've been singled out— a random act of kindness that includes an extra pat-down, a detailed luggage inspection and a few stern looks that make my palms sweat. "Why me?" I ask the navy-blue uniformed man behind the glass.

It's my unusual name, he tells me. For some reason, it's a red flag.

"I'm willing to call myself Jane if it makes things easier for everyone," I reply. He doesn't care for my humor.

When we finally board the plane, I take a window seat and watch other passengers squeeze by, lift luggage into the over-heads and pound their bags inside. So far the view is all heads: various sizes and shapes with hair that is smooth and straight or gray and fuzzy. Nothing noteworthy is happening, but I feel myself stiffening as I anticipate the doors closing and our bod-ies collectively rising above the clouds. What if there's a lunatic on this plane? There's bound to be a lunatic on this plane. I glance around, looking for the one who will potentially take us out. I'm questioning everyone. Wes catches me worrying, shoots me a look that says, "We got this." I take a deep breath, shut my eyes. When I open them again the air has changed. I'd guess that we're not moving but a look out my window says we are. Either we're drifting or everything else is shrink-ing. People, cars, buildings, stretches of road and lawn. Eve-rything is doll-sized. Smaller, smaller, gone. The sky is a sunlit opal as we soar through a mist of clouds. Then there is blue. Endless blue. I am dizzy with delight. Why have I waited so long to fly?

A year later, we board another plane to the Bahamas. On the beach at night, we sprawl out in a pair of Adirondack chairs we dragged into the water. The spectacular, gaping mouth of the ocean could swallow us whole. White-tipped waves rise and fall into oblivion. We watch jolts of lightning illuminate the sky. The world vacillates from utter blackness to a beautiful, electric expanse. It's like a child has found the light switch and cannot stop flickering the thing.

"This is amazing," I say. My voice is so small it surprises me. Wes's fingers crawl over to mine and our hands fold together like a prayer. We're not religious but tonight, we have a front-row seat on a pew.

Drip

On a Monday morning when KJ is 21, he calls to invite us to church — a Christmas Eve service.

"Okay," I say, suppressing the groan that's scaling my insides. It's been a while since I sat through a sermon, but I realize this is not about religion anymore. So when Sunday arrives, I feign enthusiasm. My son is a taller, meatier version of the boy I used to take to church, bearded yet boyish with a smile that still spells mischief. We make our way through the double doors, past the pretty young greeters who flash their lip-glossy smiles. We stop in front of an enormous Christmas tree whose red, green and gold globes gleam on lush branches. Everything twinkles. Wes and I lean in, snap a picture of ourselves then another of KJ and Anna. We shuffle into the sanctuary, a black expanse, strung with Edison bulbs so high above our heads they could be actual stars.

We sway to the music: "Joy to The World," and other Christmas tunes that make me teary-eyed and surprisingly nostalgic as I stand beside my man-son.

The service unfolds like all the others. Babies screech, the offering plate bobs about in a sea of hands and the pastor greets the congregation from the lectern. He talks about travel, about packed roads and bustling airports. Tis the season to go home, he says. Everyone wants to go home. Home.

Home to God? Home to a feeling of belonging, a sense of security, a place of acceptance? He talks about all of these things and I think of my little paper ship and the groan I have worked to suppress.

"The parable of the prodigal son is one of the greatest stories of coming home," the pastor says. "An illustration of God's forgiveness for those who lose their way."

My hands shake. My ship glides in the wet of new tears. I look around and nobody's crying but me. I try to be discreet, to mop up my cheeks with my sleeves. It's not that I am homeward bound, that my soul-ship has found a shore inside this church. It's KJ, his radiant face next to mine. That face from the past, from a morning that could have been this morning. I imagine him with an armful of toys, ushering Sym out of the kitchen saying, "Quiet, Mom's in a meeting with God."

This time, it's me who stands at the threshold of the room, and my son is alight with prayer.

Drop

I am 40, curled up in bed with Wes, the man I will marry next year. We have a home, a love, and a rhythm that feels safe and nourishing. He is not the man I feared I might find when I set up my online dating profile five years ago—he is neither commitment-phobic nor clingy. He leaves love notes on the counter, scribbled on yellow Post-its: *Happy Monday, Beautiful. Thanks for another great weekend. Love u!* He fills my car tires with air and fries my eggs just right, their sunny centers beaming in perfect circles. He is asleep and the soft whistle of his breath sweeps warmth into the hollow of my neck. I am thinking, replaying the years on the reel of my memory as the rain comes down like a heavenly gift, each drop a wet promise to cleanse, renew, refresh. I marvel at the path I have taken, the often potholed, uncertain path. I have arrived with a few calluses and a bit of dust on my feet, but I am happy and whole. There were times I searched so hard for answers, my eyes blurred to the simple truths in front of me. There were things I gripped so fiercely, my hands went numb in my skin. Things I wanted too much, prayed for and sacrificed myself for in unimaginable ways. But lying here now, I am grateful I didn't get my way. Sometimes life gives us what we need instead of what we want. I have learned that the years are the very best teachers, and they've taught me the meaning of love, family, motherhood, womanhood, and what it takes to rebuild a life.

Tonight, the moon is a wild bright eye, and it shines in through the bedroom window like a mother observing her sleeping children. My boys are men now, with jobs and facial hair, thick and bristly. Sym is in his bedroom down the hall and KJ is at his home with his wife. I hope they hear the rain tonight and feel it as I do, pulsating like the heartbeat of many memories, playing its sacred, melodic hymn.

Acknowledgements

Sometimes things come together magically. More often, they don't. It's the reason writers have editors, critique partners, and beta readers. Here's where I thank those folks.

When I came to Jill Swenson (Swenson Book Development), I had a collection of essays and ideas. As my developmental editor, she helped me find the structure and arc of this book. She asked hard questions, urged me to probe inward, find the threads that tied the past to the present and weave my narrative into a full-blown memoir. She never spared the rod, or rather the editing pen. It's a hard thing to scrutinize your own life, and to make it a published book is harder still. Excruciating even. But in the end, it is worth it. Thanks for the journey.

To Ian Andrew and the Book Reality team, thank you for your professionalism and support. Here's to the first of many great publishing adventures together (fingers crossed)!

To friends and critique partners Anita Brienza, C.C. Gallo, Jeanann Hand, I cherish your friendship and feedback. Your art has inspired my art. I hope mine has done the same for you.

To my long-gone grandma, and all the family members who have tirelessly championed my efforts; to a few great school teachers whose encouragement still echoes in my heart, I treasure you always. And to my readers, bloggy buddies and everyone who will ever connect with the lines I write, thank you for showing up and showing love. May we use our collective energy to create beautiful things, to mold pain into art that heals our hearts, heals the world.

Lastly, I thank the editors at The Sunlight Press and Literary Mama for publishing similar versions of a few of the essays in this book.

A Note To Readers

Thank you for reading this book. There are lots of beautiful stories in the world, so I am honored you chose to read mine. If you have enjoyed the journey, please leave your feedback on Amazon, Goodreads or Bookbub. Reviews are immensely appreciated.

For those who want to read more from me, please find me online at Ricawrites.com. I have so much more to share with you!

About the Author

Rica Keenum's interest in literature began in childhood, as did her author status. Armed with a set of markers and a stack of paper, she constructed her first book at age 9 -- a best seller in the making, according to her grandma. Although that book didn't garner commercial success, Rica continued to read and write and dream about reading and writing. As an adult, she landed in the medical field and worked there for more than a decade. The creative flame still burning inside her, she eventually segued to a freelance writing career by pitching articles to magazines and media companies. In 2009, she relocated to Florida with her sons and began living the final chapters of what would be her memoir, a tale of love, loss, and resilience.

She currently works as a senior staff writer for an award-winning lifestyle magazine and is pondering her next book. When not writing, she's probably reading, practicing yoga, smooching her dog or sneaking chocolate almonds out of the kitchen cabinet, so as not to alert her chocolate-loving husband.